THE
BINGO
THEORY

A revolutionary guide to love,
life, and relationships.

MIMI IKONN

Published by Dreamers & Creators Ltd.
ISBN 978-0-9954604-0-9
MIMI IKONN

Illustration by Alina Grinpauka

www.mimiikonn.com

CONTENTS

.....

DEDICATION

.....

To Alex Ikonn.

My best friend and life partner.
Thank you for coming into my life and teaching
me what true unconditional love means.

I love you for eternity and beyond.

P.S. You are my Bingo <3

ACKNOWLEDGEMENTS

. . . . .

THIS BOOK would have never come to life if it wasn't for the encouragement and contribution of so many people.

First and foremost I would like to thank my soulmate and life partner, Alex, with your support I believe anything is possible. Our loving, unconditional and effortless relationship has played a significant role in my desire to write The Bingo Theory. Thank you for not letting me give up on this book in my moments of despair and being my lighthouse in moments of darkness. My parents, Lala and Suleyman, whose relationship I have researched and observed since I can remember myself. My sister, Leyla, for always believing in my crazy ideas and providing a helping hand when needed. My dearest friend, Aysel Musayeva, with whom I spent countless hours talking about love and relationships. It is our endless conversations that lead to the idea of this book.

UJ Ramdas, a close friend and a business partner who always encourages me to get outside of my comfort zone. Thank you UJ, for pushing me into creating this body of work and also providing your valuable guidance throughout the whole process. Also, I would like to thank my friends, Jerome Jarre and Tai Lopez, who both believed in The Bingo Theory as soon as they heard about it and urged me to write this book.

After my family and friends, there is a talented team of people who have helped me create this book. I remember the day we talked about the idea of the Bingo Theory over dinner with Marianne Power, I knew she was going to help me write this book. I am so grateful that Marianne took on this project and helped me make this book a reality. I would like to thank our talented illustrator, Alina Grinpauka for creating beautiful illustrations for the book and my assistant at the time, Zane Jurjane for being my right hand in this project.

A super special thanks to all the people who have shared their life stories for the purpose of the research of this book and are presented as the case studies. You know who you are, I am deeply grateful for all of you and the contribution you have made to The Bingo Theory.

Lastly, I would like to thank the idea of this book for choosing me to bring it into this world. I am truly honored you have selected me, we had a lot of fun together and now it is time to set you free. Thank you for changing my life and my world.

"The Pentacle — The ancients envisioned their world in two halves — masculine and feminine. Their gods and goddesses worked to keep a balance of power. Yin and Yang. When male and female were balanced, there was harmony in the world. When they were unbalanced there was chaos."

— DAN BROWN, THE DA VINCI CODE

INTRODUCTION

ARE YOU THE KIND of person who finds it hard to sit still and relax? Do you feel lazy and guilty if you're not working through a to-do list? Do you pride yourself on this? Are you secretly a control freak who likes everything to go your way—yet you often feel stressed, anxious and restless?

Or perhaps your issues are just the opposite. Is inaction your problem? Do you struggle to get your life sorted out? Do you find it hard to stand up for yourself and know what to do next? Are your finances a mess? Do you constantly doubt yourself?

I believe that most people in the world fall into one of those two camps. They either can't stop or they can't get going. They're either controlling or chaotic.

Knowing which camp you fall into, will reveal a lot about your strengths and your weaknesses in your relationships. And, let's face it, you didn't pick up this book because everything is going perfect in your life, did you?

So which of these two camps are you in?

***

Every single human on this planet has two energies living within them: the masculine and the feminine.

The masculine energy helps us to operate in the outer world; it makes us strong, independent, and confident.

The feminine energy, on the other hand, helps us love and connect to others. It's what makes us creative and intuitive.

However, for most of us, one of these energies will be stronger in us—and this has a huge effect on how we approach the world.

If you have more of the masculine energy, you will be the kind of person who finds it hard to stop. You're probably ambitious, hard-working and logical, but you can also be a bit of a judgmental control freak.

On the other hand, if you have a lot of feminine energy, you are caring and fun but you find it hard to get your act together. And you can be a push over. You struggle to make decisions and get things done.

All of this has nothing to do with your biological sex. You can be a man with a lot of feminine energy and you can be a woman with a lot of masculine energy.

This is just energy. Yin and yang.

This book is about how to balance the masculine and feminine energies within you so that you can live life to the fullest.

I call this a Bingo.
Why Bingo?

Well, we've all played the game and some of us have had the joy of being able to shout out "Bingo!" when we've had that winning combination.

That's what this is about—having the winning combination of masculine and feminine energy.

This combination makes you a winner in life. It makes you the fullest version of yourself. You can then look at yourself in the mirror and feel at peace with what you see, because you have a much deeper understanding and acceptance of who you are.

It also makes you a winner in love.

Think about it. Romantically, women will say they want a man who is strong and ambitious, yet kind and sensitive. Men want a woman who is sexy and playful, yet down to earth and intelligent. What they're describing is a Bingo!

Don't you want to be someone's Bingo? Do you want to find someone who makes you so excited you want to yell "Bingo!" when they walk in the room? This isn't just about bedding someone. It's about really being with someone—the right someone—by using the principles of masculine and feminine energies.

In this book you will:
- Discover the groundbreaking medical research that has proven that, biologically, we are all a blend of masculine and feminine strengths.
- Take a quiz that helps you to determine if your strength energy is masculine or feminine. This alone is a huge eye opener. It will allow you to see clearly what amaz-

ing strengths you posses and will also highlight the areas you need to work on.

- Learn simple, actionable tips to help you balance your energies.
- Learn how to attract a Bingo relationship if you are single.
- Learn how to transform your existing relationships (whether romantic or otherwise) using the principles of masculine and feminine energies.

How to read this book

Throughout this book I will refer to four different types of people:

- Feminine Strength Female
- Feminine Strength Male
- Masculine Strength Female
- Masculine Strength Male

When I say "strength", I mean that this is your dominant energy. I refer to it as your strength because that is what it is—when used wisely.

I strongly suggest reading this book from cover to cover, including the sections that do not describe your own type. We are all a mixture of masculine and feminine energy. When you learn about other types it will give you insights into your family and friends and make it easier to relate to other types.

I use heterosexual relationships in this book but the same dynamics of masculine and feminine energy apply to all kinds of relationships—whether they are gay, trans, friendship or even family relationships.

This is just the start.

We live in changing times and we are in a state of flux when it comes to gender roles. Much has changed since the women's liberation movement took hold, and yet so many damaging stereotypes still exist: girls are still under great pressure to look a certain way and boys are told they must be strong and not show their feelings.

I believe that life becomes much simpler when we accept that we are all a blend of masculine and feminine energies. Men are not from Mars and women are not from Venus. We are all from Planet Earth. The sooner we realize that, the greater freedom, power and love we will experience—not just for ourselves, but for the world.

So let's get going…

PART ONE

Evaluating Your Masculine and Feminine Energy

.....

"If any human being is to reach full maturity, both the masculine and feminine sides of the personality must be brought up into consciousness."

— M. ESTHER HARDING

CHAPTER I

THE HISTORY OF MASCULINE
AND FEMININE ENERGY

AT THE BEGINNING of time there was only chaos. This chaos had no form but it was contained within an egg, just waiting to become something. Then one day it happened—the egg broke in two. The lighter part rose to the top to become the sky and heaven, while the heavier part sank to become the earth and the sea.

According to the Chinese creation myth, the sky was named "Yang", and represented all the masculine energy in the world. It was dry, warm and powerful.

The earth, with its moist, cooling, nourishing waters, was named "Yin" and represented all the feminine energy in the world.

Together they were a harmonious whole. Masculine and feminine, Yin and Yang. Neither was more important than the other: they were two sides of the same coin. One could not exist without the other.

If you look at the Yin and Yang symbol, each side contains a small part of the other. Within the light, Yang, masculine side is a dot of Yin, and within the dark, feminine, Yin side is a dot of Yang. We are both. The idea that we have both masculine and feminine energies within us has existed throughout history.

The ancient Mayans divided the world into masculine and feminine energies. For the Mayans, the feminine energy was the energy of caring, sharing and nurturing, as well as respect for nature, animals, plants, and all material and non-material aspects of the universe. The masculine energy, on the other hand, was the energy concerned with the material aspects of life such as striving, achieving, building and competing.

In the yoga traditions, the masculine energy—the sun—is called Shiva, and is the form or linear structure of the Universe. The feminine energy—the moon—is called Shakti and is the movement or circular force of the Universe.

Buddhists believe the right side of our brain is feminine and the left is masculine. The left hemisphere of the brain is our rational side—responsible for language, logic, math and facts. The right hemisphere is our intuitive, big-picture side. It's where our creative process starts.

Eastern philosophy believes that our quest in life is to balance both of these parts of us—the masculine and feminine, the Yin and Yang, the Sun and the Moon, Shiva and Shakti. Only then do we experience pure peace and harmony, power and love.

Carl Jung and Western Thought
The idea of masculine and feminine isn't just a spiritual concept.

In the West, the psychiatrist Carl Jung explained that men have a feminine side (which he called the 'anima') and women have a masculine side (the 'animus'). He taught that our journey in life involves coming to terms with both of these sides of ourselves.

He believed men are the physical embodiment of the masculine, yet they have the feminine energy within them. Likewise, women are the physical embodiment of the feminine, yet they have the masculine energy within them.

According to Jung, in order for a person to become whole – a process he called 'individuation' – a person must encounter and embrace both their masculine and feminine energies.

It's Biology, Baby

You can also see this concept in biology. We all come from a sperm and an egg. At the very beginning we have both masculine and feminine energy within us.

For years it was believed that men and women's brains are wired differently – the 'Men are from Mars, Women are from Venus' idea – but now a growing body of research shows that neurologically we are all a mixture of both masculine and feminine traits.

Professor Simon Baron-Cohen, a psychologist at Cambridge University, believes that we are all on a spectrum between Empathizers or Systemizers.

Systemizers are people who enjoy breaking down and analyzing systems, focusing closely on one task – what I would describe as a very masculine energy. Empathizers, on the other hand, are great at empathizing with others and communicating well—which is in line with what I call the feminine energy.

According to Baron-Cohen's research, 44 percent of women have empathizing brains, 17 percent of women have systemizing brains and 35 percent of women have brains that are roughly balanced between the two poles.

So far as men are concerned, Baron-Cohen found that 53 percent of men have systemizing brains, 17 percent have empathizing brains, and 24 percent are roughly balanced. The remaining 6 percent have an extreme male brain -- and these men, he believes, exhibit behavior that has been labeled as autistic.

Apparently, these differences are created in the womb according to how much testosterone you are exposed to as a fetus. Lots of testosterone in your mother's womb causes your brain to develop a Systemizing approach to life. Less testosterone in the womb leads to an Empathizing approach.

Evolutionary Energies

Some scientists believe that there may be an evolutionary explanation for the masculine and feminine differences.

In pre-historic society, men were hunters. Hunting requires the ability to select a target and zero in on the kill without distraction. Testosterone programs the brain for this kind of tunnel vision and focus.

On the other hand, women were the gatherers. They not only looked after the children and foraged for food but they also had to be alert to the possibilities of predators in the village. These jobs require a broader vision and the ability to communicate with other people, to sense their emotions.

A Unique Mosaic

A new way of thinking suggests that hormonal differences play a very small part in why we are the way we are.

The latest research, conducted by Daphna Joel, a professor of neuroscience at Tel Aviv University, has found that we are all a mosaic of masculine and feminine features.

Joel analyzed the brain scans of more than 1400 men and women and failed to find consistent differences between the sexes. Instead she found that we are all a unique mixture of male and female features. Her study discovered that between zero and eight percent of people had all male or all female brains. The vast majority of people were somewhere in the middle, showing that gender isn't binary – we are all a blend.

Societal Pressures

The current thinking is that men and women are more alike neurologically than they are different – it's mostly conditioning that makes us behave differently. From the moment we are born we pick up messages from our family and from society at large about how we should behave.

Psychologists believe that babies can detect whether they are boys or girls—and have also learned how to behave accordingly—by the time they are 10 months old.

Studies have shown that parents view and treat babies entirely differently depending on whether they are a boy or a girl. When a boy cries he is described as angry, whereas when a girl cries she is scared. Baby boys get spoken to and hugged much less than baby girls – isn't that sad? This then affects how they act in the world. They learn early on that they are on their own.

According to recent studies, Biology does play a part, but our brain constantly changes based on the environment we are in, a feature called neuroplasticity. Because of this, we adapt and behave according to how we think we should behave.

Traditionally boys are encouraged to express more masculine energy, and this reinforces a sense of masculinity. We see this when boys kick and push on the playground. This might come naturally—or it might not.

As a result of societal pressures, a sensitive boy who is raised in a house where it is believed that men have to be strong, unemotional and aggressive, might go on to copy this masculine approach. The alternative for such a boy is to get laughed at for wanting to play with girls or wanting to do activities that are considered feminine.

Similarly, most families and cultures encourage girls to express more of the feminine energy. They are taught to be gentle and caring with each other, to talk and to listen.

As a result of such pressures, a girl who loves to run around and play rough with the boys might understand early on that this is not what she should be doing. Instead she should be playing with dolls and talking to other girls.

Furthermore, as children grow up their parent's dominant energy continues to influence them.

For example, you might have a stronger feminine energy but if you were raised by a Masculine Strength Parent who was hugely ambitious career-wise and wanted you to follow the same path, there is a good chance you will go on to adopt that masculine energy, particularly at work.

The family, culture, religion and society we're raised in greatly influences which energy we express more of, as well as when and how we express that energy.

So which energy have you learned to express more of? Which is your dominant – or strength energy?

Take our tests to find out…

"We are born male or female, but not masculine or feminine."

— SANDRA BARTKY

2

ASSESSING YOUR UNIQUE BALANCE

So far we've discussed the idea that we each have both masculine and feminine energy but as a result of hormones, upbringing and societal influences, one of these energies will be more dominant in each of us. Which energy is dominant is not necessarily related to your biological sex – you can be a man with a strong feminine energy or a woman with a strong masculine energy. Or you can be a woman with a strong feminine energy or a man with a strong masculine energy.

So which is your dominant energy? Do you have a feeling already?

In a minute you will take a quiz to help you determine your dominant energy, but first here is a very quick and fun test to get you going.

The Finger Test
Flatten out your right hand and take a look at your fingers, in particular your index finger (next to your thumb)

Feminine

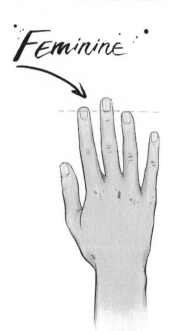

Masculine

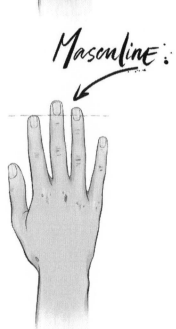

and your ring finger (next to your little finger).

Which is longer?

It can be quite subtle, but Masculine Strength People tend to have ring fingers (measured from the crease where the finger joins the hand) that are longer than their index fingers. People with Feminine Strength tend to have ring fingers and index fingers of the same length, or they have index fingers that are longer.

Why? Well, scientists have found that the more testosterone you are exposed to in the womb, the longer your ring finger will be. As we have seen already, testosterone is the hormone linked to masculine energy. On the other hand, the index finger indicates the estrogen levels in a person.

Keep in mind that from my personal research, I found that this hand test is very effective at instantly indicating a person's strength energy, however it is not 100% accurate. There were some exceptions.

Strengths Quiz

Next, get a pen and take a look at the characteristics below. Which words jump out at you? Which ones describe your approach to life?

Circle exactly ten of these characteristics that you believe to be your natural strengths. In other words, these are things that come naturally to you, things you rely on every day.

Follow your first instincts. When doing this quiz only pick the things that you are actually good at—do not pick characteristics that you would like to believe you are good at, or ones that you want to get better at. Go with your gut and don't overthink it.

The more honest you are with yourself the better and more accurate your feedback will be.

If you have a hard time picking your strengths, I would suggest you think about your closest friends and family. We are usually the most authentic with them. How would they describe you? When you see your reflection through the eyes of those who know you well, you can begin to identify your personal talents.

For example: I am empathetic, although empathy is not my strength. Is it something I am working on? Sure! But I have to be honest with myself. It's not my natural strength. One of my strength is "Active." I'm always moving, always doing something. I have a hard time sitting still.

Now, choose your ten strengths:

---

1. Flexible	11. Competitive
2. Active	12. Empathetic
3. Direct	13. Reliable
4. Expressive	14. Free-spirited
5. Ambitious	15. Creative
6. Nurturing	16. Rebelious
7. Sensitive	17. Decisive
8. Trusting	18. Gentle
9. Strong	19. Intuitive
10. Confident	20. Logical

Now, look below and add up the points you have earned for each of the words you circled.

ANSWERS

1. 5	11. 1
2. 1	12. 5
3. 1	13. 1
4. 5	14. 5
5. 1	15. 5
6. 5	16. 1
7. 5	17. 1
8. 5	18. 5
9. 1	19. 5
10. 1	20. 1

RESULTS

If you scored 30 or below your strength energy is masculine. (Exception: if you are man and you scored exactly 30, your strength energy is feminine)

If you scored 31 and above your strength energy is feminine.

The lower your score, the stronger your masculine strength is. The higher the score, the stronger your feminine strength is.

So what does that mean?

What is the difference between masculine and feminine energy?

Masculine and Feminine Energy List

Masculine Energy is:

LOGICAL: It uses rational, analytical and scientific thought processes to make choices. It can be cynical and closed-minded.

CONFIDENT: It is assertive, decisive and powerful. It takes action. It is happy to take risks and also take responsibility. It can be controlling. It is always certain it is right.

COMPETITIVE: It is driven, focused, determined, disciplined, goal-oriented and ambitious. It is concerned with money and status. It can be impatient, striving, judgmental, possessive and jealous.

STRONG: It is physically strong and emotionally reliable. It is consistent and responsible, loyal, hard-working and generous.

INDEPENDENT: It seeks freedom, not connection. It is rebellious and dislikes authority. It values itself and struggles to connect with others and to express feelings.

Feminine Energy is:

EMOTIONAL: It is empathetic, kind, loving, compassionate and nurturing. It can get lost in emotions and lose sight of goals.

INTUITIVE: It is wise, introspective, creative and sensitive.

FREE-SPIRITED: It lives in the moment and is spontaneous, fun-loving and aesthetic; it can be unpredictable, unreliable, disorganized and chaotic. It is usually not good with managing money.

EXPRESSIVE: It communicates freely and easily. It connects easily with others. It can talk endlessly and in circles.

OPEN: It is open-minded, cooperative, collaborative and trusting. It is patient and receptive. It values others. It is happy to be rather than to do. It can be naïve and too easily persuaded.

3

OWN YOUR STRENGTHS

BEFORE WE MOVE ON to the next section, I'd like you to take a moment to really embrace your strength energy.

Is it masculine or feminine?

How do you feel about it?

The Feminine Energy Is Not Weak

As a modern, successful, career-driven woman, you might not like being associated with feminine energy – you might think that it's somehow sexist or patronizing. You might associate the word feminine with weakness.

You might read this and think, "But I'm strong and ambitious!" And that's great! This is the masculine energy in you coming forward. But what comes most naturally to you? What are you like when you are not at work? Are you more logical or more emotional? Do you draw first on your caring, loving side? Or do you draw first on your clear-thinking decisive side?

If you're a guy, you might want to run away from the

word feminine. You might think it implies you're girlie, or less of a man.

We live in a time that celebrates the masculine go-getting energy above all else.

Masculine Energy Does Not Make You a Macho Idiot

On the flipside, some men might think that it's no longer socially acceptable to own their masculine energy. They might think that it makes them like their aggressive, domineering fathers, and that these days all men need to show their sensitive side. That's absolutely right!

It takes a *real* man to be emotional and caring and to not care how others perceive this side of them.

Being a Masculine Strength Male or Female does not mean that you are destined to be aggressive, controlling or cut off from your feelings. You can still be open, kind and loving.

You can use your feminine energy without walking away from your natural strength—which is your clear thinking, your ambition, and your desire to make your mark on the world.

We must always remember we have BOTH energies within us. It's just that one of the energies has become more developed in us through a combination of hormones, life-experiences and conditioning.

Own Your Super Power

The trick is to OWN your natural strength, not fight it. That's when the magic happens, that's when you tap into your super powers.

If you have a dominant feminine energy, own it regardless of whether you are male or female. Tell yourself, "It's my strength to be a caring, compassionate, loving and connected person."

Likewise, if you have a strong masculine energy—regardless of whether you are male or female—own the fact that "It's my strength to be an ambitious go-getter who clearly focuses on what I want and how to get it."

It's not that you can't do other things – it's just that these things come more easily to you.

Once you know what comes to you naturally, you don't have to work on that any more. Instead, work on building up your less-dominant energy.

As mentioned previously, it is important to understand that we all have both masculine and feminine energy in us. It's just that most of us have one energy that is more developed – whether through nature or conditioning – and this often leads to an imbalance.

The purpose of this book is to balance your masculine and feminine energies so that you can enjoy a happy, healthy and balanced life.

PART TWO

The Four Types

.....

IN THE NEXT four chapters I will tell you more about my four friends. Lily and Chris are Feminine Strength People, while Chloe and Andrew are Masculine Strength People.

They have shared openly with me their strengths and struggles – I am sure you will relate to them.

Instead of just looking at masculine and feminine energy, I look at the way both energies manifest in both the sexes because the energies sometimes manifest differently depending on the sex of the person.

A great way to see the different way the energies manifest is by looking at people's sex drive.

The Masculine Strength Male has a very strong sex drive. He is always ready and open for action in the bedroom, or elsewhere!

This is not the case with a Masculine Strength Female. She's too busy getting stuff done to keep jumping into bed. She's got no time for that! Sure she likes sex as a release every now and then, but she has other priorities.

On the other hand, the Feminine Strength Female has a high sex drive. She would happily spend the weekend in bed—ideally with wine and chocolate delivered. To her sex is a vital part of a relationship – and of life. It's the time when she expresses her love and, indeed, herself.

The Feminine Strength Male prioritizes intimacy and connection over sex. He is happy with a kiss and a cuddle on the sofa and is usually comfortable to admit that he does not have a very strong sex drive. Well...not as strong as Masculine Strength males that is.

Another way to see the differences is by looking at their physical form. The Feminine Strength Male tends to be slender while the Feminine Strength Female is generally curvy, for example.

You probably want to read your type first if you haven't already. But when you've done that I suggest that you read through all the profiles.

Remember that we are all a mixture of masculine and feminine energy. Therefore, you might recognize yourself in some of the other profiles as well. More importantly, they will help you better relate to strengths and struggles that other people in your life have. They might also help you understand why your best friend has more highs and lows than a roller coaster, for example. Or why your father is unable to say more to you than -"How is work?"

To begin with, I will describe what these types are like when they're single. Later in the book we'll see how they operate in relationships. Even if you are in a relationship, please read the first chapters. They are the core chapters that will help you to understand your strengths and your challenges. They'll explain your approach to relationships, work, and the world in general. I promise you it's an eye-opener! A lot of things will become clear.

Lastly, I should warn you that not everything will be a perfect fit. But if you feel connected to one of the personality types, trust your instincts. Don't think about it too much. Just take what works for you and leave the rest.

So, are you ready?

CHAPTER IV

FEMININE STRENGTH
FEMALE

LET'S START with the Feminine Strength Female.

In many ways, she is the embodiment of what society thinks women should be like. She's kind, caring, loving and sensitive. She is more interested in being a nice person than a successful person. She puts others before herself.

These are all wonderful qualities. But being nice isn't easy in a world that encourages competition, ambition, pushing harder and faster. It's very easy for the Feminine Strength Female to have her good nature taken advantage of and she often finds it hard to take control of her life – and her finances.

Let me tell you about my friend, Lovely Lily.

Lily enjoys her work writing for an interior design magazine. She gets to look at pretty things, talk to interesting people and write, which she has always loved.

She's been in the same position for five years and she knows she should be climbing the ladder but she doesn't want the extra responsibility of a bigger job.

Sometimes this makes her feel like a loser – most of her friends from college are doing so well in their careers. She knows she isn't built like them. It's not that she's not intelligent enough – far from it. In school she was a diligent, straight A student. But career-wise she isn't that ambitious. She doesn't see the point in spending life climbing up a ladder. We're all going to die, so who cares whether you've got letters after your name or if you ran a company?

Lily was never competitive. Even at school, when it came to sports she hated that someone had to lose. Why can't we all win? Why does it matter who comes first or last? Or who earns the most?

Lily just wants to get along with everyone – and she does. She has always found it easy to make friends and is one of those people that everybody likes. She is also one of those lucky souls who can walk into a party and strike up a conversation with anyone.

But while she can be a social butterfly, Lily is also a home bird who loves her apartment. Her favorite thing to do on the planet is to lay in the bath or lounge on the sofa. She's also happy to sit in a coffee shop watching the world. She's not one of those people who finds it hard to relax. Hard to get going, yes, but hard to relax, no. Her friends joke that Lily could spend days just looking out a window.

Lily likes the finer things in life – beautiful clothes, lovely furniture, dinners out. She has a bit of a shopping habit.

There are a lot of great things in Lily's life, but underneath it all the cracks are showing.

She tells herself that life is too short to worry about money and that it's important to look her best – something her glamorous mother instilled in her. But she frequently runs out of money before payday and her credit card bills are mounting.

Lily should ask for a raise at work but she hates such conversations. She's not very good at standing up for herself - either in her work or in her private life. She finds it hard to say no and often ends up going along with what other people want to do.

Lily often has the feeling that she doesn't know what she's doing in life. It's like she's waiting for something to happen, which she is. The truth is, she'd really like to get married and have children. She knows it's not acceptable to say it these days, but she'd like to be a full-time mom.

Although Lily dates a lot, she hasn't met the right guy yet. She sees the best in people but friends say she is a poor judge of character. Her last boyfriend consistently cheated on her but she didn't break up with him for months. He kept begging for forgiveness and she kept thinking he would change. She hated herself for being such a cliché. Finally, she broke up with him but she hasn't met anyone better since. She doesn't know why but she keeps attracting the kind of men who are only after one thing.

If you met Lily socially, you would probably think she's one of those blessed people who has it all. She's pretty, well-dressed, popular and easy-going. She goes through life with a smile on her face. But what's going on inside her is a different matter. Lily has real anxiety. She feels lost and overwhelmed. And she doubts herself and her abilities because she knows that she can be too trusting of other people, especially men.

Here are some of the traits of the Feminine Strength Female:

Empathetic

The greatest gift of the Feminine Strength Female is her ability to love, connect, nurture and build relationships. When Lily walks into a room, pretty much everyone in it will like her. Making friends is something that comes so easily to her that she doesn't realize how much other people struggle with it.

The Feminine Strength Female cares deeply about people—so much so that she tends to put other people's needs before their own. She is also hugely empathetic and nurturing. She has an innate ability to read people's feelings and respond appropriately. She can relate to others on a very deep, human level. Perhaps unsurprisingly, then, her priority is relationships – not work.

Free-spirited

The Feminine Strength Female doesn't define herself by her job. She's more of a free-spirit. Lily is conscientious and works hard, but she keeps passing up promotions even though she needs the money. Why? She doesn't want the extra responsibility and neither the status nor the impressive job title mean anything to her. As for office politics? Forget it. Life's too short. She wants to enjoy life, not spend it stressed out.

Emotional

The Feminine Strength Female lives in a world of feelings and introspection. She's the kind of person whose eyes well up when she sees an old lady cross the road. She loves nothing more than going through a whole box of tissues during a weepie movie. She is very sensitive to trauma. She still hasn't got over the horror movie she watched with her ex-boyfriend. "Why on earth do you like this?" she asked him. "It's not real," he laughed. But everything is real to the Feminine Strength Female, who feels everything deeply. She has the emotional capacity of a roller coaster – she can be high as a kite one minute and in the depths of despair the next.

Expressive

The Feminine Strength Female has no problems sharing her feelings – there is no bottling up for her. That's what her Masculine Strength Friends do. She feels no shame about crying in public and will express herself to friends at length. She loves long phone calls and can endlessly analyze life with her friends over cups of tea and glasses of wine. If you ask a Feminine Strength Female how her day is, she'll still be talking about it an hour later.

Relaxed

The Feminine Strength Female lives in a gentle way. While her Masculine Strength friends run around, striving and hustling, she sits still and lives in the moment. She doesn't need to do anything... she is happy just to be. She can spend the whole weekend on the sofa and hours in the bath—sensual pleasures are important to her. Her Masculine Strength friends are baffled by her, ability to do nothing. "Aren't you bored?!" they want to know. Well, no. The Feminine Strength Female rarely gets bored. And while she loves people's company, she also relishes time on her own. She doesn't need outside distraction to make her feel OK.

Creative

The Feminine Strength Female—and the Feminine Strength Male, for that matter—has a keen sense of beauty and enjoys the finer things in life. Art, design and interior decor are all important to her. So too is fashion. She sees it as a form of self-expression. She has confidence in her outfits and loves to make a statement. She's the kind of woman who can put on a crazy outfit from a vintage store and make it look fabulous.

Curvaceous

Lily has been told she has the body of a pin-up, and that's typical of the Feminine Strength Female. Estrogen, the female hormone, causes weight to distribute to the buttocks and hips, creating the classic hourglass shape. (Testosterone, the male hormone that is likely higher in Masculine Strength Females, encourages fat to form around the waist, creating a more up- and- down figure). Estrogen also reduces the size of the nose and chin, in-

creases the size of the eyes and the thickness of the lips;
It also creates plump cheeks.

Lacking Direction

So what are Lily's struggles? One of the biggest issues for
the Feminine Strength Female is a lack of direction. This
makes it possible for her to go with the flow and be spontaneous, but it can also make her feel lost at times. She
finds it hard to make decisions and to structure her time,
to plan, or to move towards goals. Everywhere she goes
she see options. She get swayed in a million directions.
She can feel aimless and out of control a lot of the time –
especially when it comes to her finances.

Struggles With Money Management

The Feminine Strength Female is the kind of person who
puts unopened bank statements in her drawer. She sees
her credit card limits as a target to hit—rather than a place
you should never get to. Nobody who lives for the moment, as she does, worries about savings. How boring!

Although the Feminine Strength Female is talented
and creative she does not monetize her talents well. This
could be because she does not value herself enough. It
could also be because she does not like talking about
money. Like Lily, she is unlikely to ask for pay rises. If
she runs her own business she won't charge as much as
she should. She pretends that money doesn't matter but
she certainly likes the finer things in life. Underlying
her apparently carefree attitude is a fear of facing up to
financial realities and taking control (taking control is

very much part of the masculine energy). Deep down she may be waiting for someone to come and rescue her.

Hates Confrontation

The Feminine Strength Female is by nature, a people pleaser, a diplomat, and she will do anything to avoid confrontation. She'll never just say directly what she thinks or needs. She won't use blunt language such as No or Stop it. Instead, she'll say things like "Would you mind...err...please, not doing that...?" Or she'll say nothing at all. She'll almost always put other people's needs before her own.

Picks The Wrong Guys

We'll talk about this more in later chapters, but one of the downsides of the Feminine Strength Female's open-heart and trusting nature is that she gets sucked in by the wrong guys. As a result of her good looks and fun personality she has no problem getting men. But because she does not stand up for herself, she often gets treated like a doormat or ends up being just another notch in the bedpost.

Can You Relate?

Do you recognize any of Lily's traits in yourself? Do you find it easy to make friends? Do you love to live in the moment and enjoy the beauty in everything? Do you see yourself run around to please others without the courage to please yourself? Do you find it hard to organize your life and plan ahead? Are you very sensitive? Do you lack career ambition?

If you're a Feminine Strength Female you might read this now and feel angry: Isn't talk about not valuing your career just sexist nonsense? Is Mimi suggesting we all go back to the 1950s? No, I'm not suggesting that at all. I am just explaining that different energies have different priorities.

In today's world we've been brain-washed to think that careers are everything. But climbing the corporate ladder is not for everyone. The fact is that not all people want the same things.

There are a lot of Feminine Strength Females (and Males) who feel badly because the world tells them they should be an entrepreneur or a CEO. As a result of this persistent messaging, they think there is something wrong with them because they don't want that. Well, there isn't. The world needs all kinds of people.

Career, status and success are important to Masculine Strength People. But they are not as important to Feminine Strength People, who prioritize other values like family, health and relationships.

There are, of course, many exceptions. If you are a Feminine Strength Female that has been brought up in a family where career was important, that attitude may have rubbed off on you.

Not all Feminine Strength Females are the same. Also, there is a spectrum of femininity – just as there is a spectrum of masculinity. Because of this, you might fall on the extreme end—as Lily does—or you may be more balanced, with more masculine energy in you.

It's important to understand that we all have both

masculine and feminine energy in us. You don't just have one or the other energy – you have both. It's just that for most of us one of these energies will be more developed – whether through nature or conditioning. I will keep repeating this throughout the book because it's very important that you understand this.

The purpose of this book is to balance your masculine and feminine energies so that you can draw on both energies equally and thus lead a full and balanced life.

CHAPTER V

FEMININE STRENGTH MALE

THE FEMININE STRENGTH MALE is one of my favorite kind of people – I even married one! Fun, creative, romantic, stylish—they are great guys to spend time with. But what's behind the cool outfits and easy smile? Let me tell you about my dear friend Chris...

Chris is a graphic designer and works for a small company. He likes his job but it's not what he wants to do forever. In fact, he has a couple of business ideas – they just haven't gotten off the ground yet. For now, the job helps him earn enough money to pay the bills.

Chris is popular at work. Everybody loves him. He's funny, sweet and lighthearted. He's the one to cheer people up when they're stressed. He sends them silly emails or draws them little pictures. He makes them tea. All the women in the office love him – and he loves them. They joke that he's one of the girls and he's fine with that.

Even as a kid, Chris was very relaxed with women. He

was very close to his mother and his two sisters—and was scared of his bullying, aggressive father. In fact, he decided early on in life that he was going to be nothing like his father.

At school Chris was never one of the jocks who was into girls and ran around the football field. His guy friends never understood how he was so comfortable with girls—but none of them were his girlfriend. "Are you gay?" they'd tease. He wasn't. Not at all. He just liked female company and didn't see what the big deal was.

For a while Chris tried to be more like the other guys. He started smoking and drinking. He even got into weight lifting to feel more manly. He's naturally very slender but he tried to bulk up because that's what girls seemed to like. He drank protein shakes non-stop.

Now he's given up on all that. He accepted who he is and now gets by on his wicked sense of humor and great style. And he really does have great style. He knows the pale blue sweaters bring out the color of his eyes. And he's living testimony to the fact the modern men moisturize. He also has no problem having a cocktail or a glass of wine—beer never really did it for him.

Despite the fact that Chris has so much going for him—he has moments when he's quite insecure. He doubts himself and he over-thinks things. He can feel down and overwhelmed. His biggest struggle is that he doesn't know what he wants out of life. It feels like there are so many paths he could go down and he doesn't know which one to pick. He finds it hard to stick to things and to follow through. He has lots of great ideas but rarely

makes any of them happen. His father always said he was a starter, not a finisher—and he was right.

Chris is single at the moment but he's usually in a relationship. He broke up with his last girlfriend (of four years) about a year ago and hasn't dated anyone since. He finds it hard to make the first move and usually ends up in the friend zone.

Today's world is more embracing of Feminine Strength Males than it used to be. These days it's acceptable for guys to take care of their appearance and to enjoy the finer things in life. That said, there are challenges.

A lot of Feminine Strength Males have a tough childhood. They're accused of being gay and get teased for being sensitive; for not living up to the stereotype of the Real Man. Their natural sensitivity and creativity is stamped out of them. This is heartbreaking because the Feminine Strength Male has many amazing qualities.

Here are some of his traits:

Charming

As we can see with Chris, the Feminine Strength Male is typically charming. He walks into a room and makes it come alive. Like the Feminine Strength Female, he finds it easy to talk to people and to get them to open up. He loves to communicate and can talk for hours. He's also playful and fun—although because he's shy it may take a bit of time to see this side of him. Unlike the Masculine Strength Male, the Feminine Strength Male has no desire to dominate situations.

Caring

The Feminine Strength Male is thoughtful, considerate, caring and gentle. He's patient and a natural peacemaker. He has an innate ability to be empathetic for what other people are going through. He's happy to open up and be honest about his problems and emotions. He's prepared to be vulnerable and he shows affection openly.

Stylish

The Feminine Strength Male is usually image-conscious. He loves dressing up and takes care of his appearance. He is the kind of guy that plans his outfit before he goes out. There's a good chance his socks match his sweater or his shoes have been handmade in a little place he knows. In other words, he is the classic metrosexual guy. His home is full of cool touches, such as retro film posters, great art, and even the occasional scented candle.

Cultured

The Feminine Strength Male like the arts, film and music. He's often a big reader–not of the sports pages, but of literature and poetry. He's intelligent, considerate and appreciates beauty in all its forms. He likes the finer things in life. He would rather sip on one beautiful glass of wine than neck down bottles of beer. He's likely to be a foodie.

Slender

Testosterone causes the jaw and eyebrow ridges to become prominent, it also causes a more muscular frame and broad shoulders. It's possible the Feminine Strength Male does not have such high levels of testosterone as the Masculine Strength Male, which may lead to finer features such as a rounder jaw and slim wrists. He might be on the slender side—although diet and exercise patterns will obviously influence that.

Impeccable Hygiene

The Feminine Strength Male is better scrubbed up than the average Joe. He is the kind of guy who has expensive bath oil and is living proof that real men exfoliate. He might even make an occasional trip to a spa. As for his hair, he won't just walk into any barber-shop. He will go to the trendiest hair salon his wallet can afford because he doesn't want just any barber fooling around with his hair. If there's a bit of head massage offered as part of the experience, so much the better.

Likes Female Company

The Feminine Strength Male loves female company – both for friendship and romance. He tends to be drawn to stronger women, though; ones who know what they want and take charge. He loves it when other people take control.

Creative

Creativity is where the Feminine Strength Male shines. He has great ideas, a strong design eye, and an intuitive sense of what people want. This makes him very good at predicting trends. He's an idea machine, with his finger on the pulse.

Disorganized

The main problem is that the Feminine Strength Male finds it hard to actually carry out his great ideas. It's a struggle for him to plan and to make decisions. He gets overwhelmed by options and doesn't know which way to go. When he starts something, he often loses interest half way through – something else catches his attention. He's a starter, not a finisher.

Insecure

A lot of the Feminine Strength Male's difficulties stem from his insecurity. He doubts himself in a way his Masculine Strength friends don't. He doesn't have confidence that what he does will succeed.

Talks Big

To disguise his self-doubt, the Feminine Strength Male may carry on with a lot of big talk. He draws everyone in with his exciting ideas, but the more he talks, the less likely he is to actually do anything. In extreme cases he can be quite delusional: To meet him you might think he is a multi-millionaire investor, when actually, he only has a couple of shares in his friend's company.

Needy

Deep down the Feminine Strength Male seeks approval. Instead of building himself up, he looks to others to do it. He can easily fall into victim-mode. Like the Feminine Strength Female, he may be prone to ups and downs.

Friend Zoned

The Feminine Strength Male's lack of confidence can be a big issue when it comes to dating. He has an extremely hard time making the first move. He's scared of rejection and of the embarrassing moment when he puts himself on the line. He talks himself out of it – telling himself that the woman he likes is out of his league. Instead he becomes her friend and they hang out. She's blissfully unaware that he is romantically interested. After all, if he liked her, surely he'd have asked her out by now? Right?

Can You Relate?

Do you share some of Chris's strengths and struggles? Are you a stylish guy with a load of friends? Are you busting with ideas but find it hard to follow through? Do you doubt yourself?

You may be reading this as a Feminine Strength Male and think "Slow down! I have a successful business. I know how to execute a plan and make things happen." That's great.

A lot of very successful entrepreneurs are Feminine Strength Males. They have the ideas, the charm and the intuition needed to make their business a success.

However, if you look at the Feminine Strength people who are successful, you will usually find that they work with a Masculine Strength business partner, manager or producer. They team up with someone who keeps them on track and on-budget; someone who keeps their feet on the ground. Is this the case with you?

Remember also that not all Feminine Strength Males

are the same. There is a spectrum of femininity – just as there is a spectrum of masculinity. You might fall on the extreme end, as Chris does, or you might be more balanced.

As I have said before, it's important to understand that we all have both masculine and feminine energy in us. You don't have one or the other energy – you have both. It's just that most people have one of these energies more developed – whether through nature or conditioning. I will keep repeating this point throughout the book because it's very important to understand.

The purpose of this book is to balance your masculine and feminine energies so that you can draw on both energies equally in order to lead a full, healthy and balanced life.

6

MASCULINE STRENGTH FEMALE

THE MASCULINE STRENGTH FEMALE is someone close to my heart because it's the quadrant that I fall into! Competitive, driven, ambitious and decisive, we are the type of women you'll see in the boardroom and in the gym. We push ourselves hard, but that can come at a price.

Let me tell you about my friend, Chloe.

As a child Chloe was a tomboy. She climbed trees, ran track and was always happier hanging out with boys than girls. She didn't wear her lip-gloss until she was at college. She was definitely not one of those girls who hung out in the mall. In fact, she couldn't see the point of shopping at all. What a giant waste of time!

If she had her way, Chloe would live in jeans and sweats all the time. She sees clothes as nothing more than functional. As she got older, however, she accepted that it was important to look her best. She decided that twice a year she would go shopping with a girlfriend to buy all her clothes, and that would be it – she'd be done. Life is too short to spend it in fitting rooms. It was a typical Chloe move – practical and efficient; get the job done and move on.

She had more important things to think about, like her career. After graduating near the top of her class at law school, Chloe got a job at a very big firm. She beat a lot of competition in order to get this opportunity.

Both of Chloe's parents also worked in law and were hugely successful. Growing up, she did not see them much. In her family the message was clear: work was everything.

She works long hours. She's even been known to sleep in the office. Colleagues describe her as The Machine; she just keeps going. Friends joke that her apartment looks like nobody lives in it: the fridge is always empty except for the juice and fruit that her cleaner leaves for her.

There is talk of Chloe making partner soon–which will make her one of the youngest partners in the history of her company. It all looks great from the outside, but she never feels like she's doing enough.

In her personal life, Chloe is the one that everyone relies on – she organizes her friends' birthday parties and members of her family turn to her for advice. She knows how to stay calm in a crisis. She can make decisions and isn't afraid of confrontation. People frequently describe her as their rock.

But who is there for Chloe? She's so capable nobody ever thinks that she might need support. But she does. The truth is she's having a hard time.

Chloe used to thrive on the challenges of her work and her ability to do it all but now she wakes up exhausted and anxious. She wants a holiday but work is too busy at the moment.

Friends tell Chloe she needs to relax, but who has time for that? She's tried yoga and liked it, but because of work demands she can't commit to a class every week. Instead, she runs. And she pushes herself further and further on her runs. In fact, she's training for the New York City Marathon next year.

All of Chloe's running and working and being there for everyone should make her feel complete. Instead, it keeps her so busy that she can't think about the one big hole in her life – a boyfriend. She wants to get married and start a family but it isn't happening.

Chloe's been single for the last two years. She's done some online dating but nothing serious. She finds it hard to meet her match. She thinks that guys are intimidated by her success. She jokes that she needs someone more Alpha than her–but those guys are hard to find.

If Chloe were to pick two words to describe her, the words would be intelligent and confident. And she is. The Masculine Strength Female is clear thinking, loyal and practical. She's ambitious, hard working and driven in her career. Her work means a lot to her and she's proud of the fact that she can do anything a man can do—and then some.

When you read about a female CEO who juggles long hours and family, she's probably a Masculine Strength

Female. She's focused and decisive; she gets the job done. When people say "I don't know how you do it," she'll answer, "I don't know – I just do." End of story. She doesn't have time to talk about her life, she's too busy living it.

Here are some of her traits:

Tomboy

As a child Chloe was a tomboy. She preferred male company to female company. This is very common for the Masculine Strength Female. She prefers more active, adventurous play than the more feminine activities, like talking and playing with dolls. As she gets into her teens, she tends to hang out with guys and doesn't see why other girls act so silly around the opposite sex. She also doesn't understand how her Feminine Strength friends can spend hours doing nothing more than putting on make-up.

Athletic

Like many Masculine Strength Females, Chloe is naturally athletic in her physique and in her interests – she loves running. Many Masculine Strength Females will have higher levels of testosterone than other women, and this might cause them to have broader shoulders and a straight, up-and-down body. They tend to like competitive, intense sports.

Ambitious

The Masculine Strength Female is usually very career-driven. It's not just money that motivates her though; she wants to leave her mark on the world, to smash the glass ceiling. Very often the Masculine Strength Female becomes frustrated by the sexism they perceive at work. They know they are just as capable as men, and get angry when this is not acknowledged. Both Chloe's parents were very driven in their career (they were Masculine Strength people) and so she absorbed the message that work is important.

Independent

The Masculine Strength Female wants to do things her own way. She won't follow anyone's lead. She's a bit of a rebel. She's hugely independent—in her thinking and in the way she lives. She has her own money, her own pension, and her own home. She never wants to rely on a man to provide her with anything. She can do that herself, thank you very much. She takes great strength in feeling in control over her life. She makes the decisions, she makes the plans.

Reliable

The Masculine Strength Female is reliable. She does what she says she's going to do. She sticks to the plan. She's not the kind of person to cancel at the last-minute or change her mind. If she said she'll be there, she'll be there—mind you, that also means she gets annoyed with her less reliable Feminine Strength friends when they turn up late and change plans.

Honest

While Feminine Strength Females tend to be people-pleasers, the Masculine Strength Female is honest. She's the kind of person who will tell you if your bum actually does look big in those jeans, or if you look like you're wearing a tent. This isn't always fun to hear, but her honesty makes her a wonderful friend. She has the courage to tell you things that other people won't.

Kind

The Masculine Strength Female's honesty is not bitchiness – far from it. She's a true friend. She's kind, loyal and generous. She always wants to help the people in her life. She might not spend hours listening to your problems–she doesn't have the patience for that—but she will do all she can to help in practical ways. She'll turn up with a van to help you move . She'll create spreadsheets to help you sort out your finances. She'll use her clear and logical thinking to help you assemble the most complicated flat-pack furniture. She loves the challenge. She's a doer.

Can't Relax

The problem for the Masculine Strength Female is that she does not know how to stop 'doing'. She goes to work even when she's sick. She's not the kind to sit on the sofa on the weekend. She's always off doing something. If she's not working on her to-do list, she feels lazy and unproductive. She's very hard on herself and finds it hard to relax and have fun.

Finds It Hard To Express

The Masculine Strength Female can also find it hard to

express herself, especially emotionally. She isn't one for talking for hours, and she knows that her friends sometimes wish she'd just listen to them rather than tell them what to do. At work, she has a reputation for being blunt—but she sees that as a double standard. Men get praised for being direct while she gets accused of being abrupt.

Lacks Empathy
The Masculine Strength Female (and Male) also finds it a challenge to understand and relate to other people's feelings. Friends always tell her that things are not as black and white as she makes them out to be. But she doesn't understand how other people make things so confusing and emotional. She has a brain that sees systems and solutions – not feelings. She has the systemizer brain, according to Professor Baron-Cohen's theory.

Controlling
The Masculine Strength Female can be authoritative. She gets annoyed when people don't do what she tells them to do—especially when it's in their own interest. She likes to be in control and hates it when she's not. She can also be possessive of her friends – the masculine energy likes to own things.

Impatient
The Masculine Strength Female gets impatient when things don't go her way – whether that's at work or in her personal life. When dating isn't going her way, it drives her crazy. She approaches love the same way she does every other

area in her life—as a problem she can fix with enough clear thinking. But love doesn't seem to work that way.

Can You Relate?

Do you recognize yourself in any of Chloe's behavior? Do you push yourself too hard, to the extent that you're cut off from your feelings? Are you so serious and ambitious that you've stopped taking time to relax and have fun?

Remember that not all Masculine Strength Females are the same. There is a spectrum of masculinity – just as there is a spectrum of femininity. You might fall on the extreme end, as Chloe does, or you might be more balanced.

As a Masculine Strength Female, you might argue that you are very playful and loving – and that you're not serious and focused all the time. Of course you are! That's your feminine energy coming out.

In Chloe's case, she may be impatient with friends and at work, but she is very patient, playful and nurturing with her young niece. Children and animals bring out her feminine energy. They open up her heart to love.

As I keep saying, it's important to understand that we all have both masculine and feminine energy in us. You're not one or the other energy – you're both. It's just that most of us have developed one of these energies more than the other–whether through nature or conditioning. I will keep repeating this throughout the book because it's very important that you understand this.

The purpose of this book is to balance your masculine and feminine energies so that you can draw on both energies equally in order to lead a full and healthy life.

CHAPTER VII

MASCULINE STRENGTH MALE

FINALLY, LET ME INTRODUCE YOU to my friend, Andrew, a great example of the Masculine Strength Male. When I met Andrew, he was in his late twenties and he was, to use his phrase, living the dream. He used his masculine energy to his advantage.

Andrew plays to win–he always has and always will. As the eldest of three boys, he learned early on that life is a competition and there's no prize for second place. You have to fight for your corner and fight hard. The phrases "man up" and "boys don't cry" were used often in his house.

At school Andrew played football, was on the debate team and got straight A's.

Not that studying came easy to him—he thought that most of his teachers were a waste of space and he couldn't see the point of half the classes. But he wanted to get into an Ivy League College so he figured out that the bare minimum was to get A's and that's what he did.

Andrew never saw his Old Man as proud as he was the day Andrew got accepted into Yale. It was a great moment.

For awhile at Yale he struggled. The standard was high and it was tough being around people more intelligent than he was. For once Andrew wasn't winning.

When he got his first C, he was floored. He was not used to coming so close to failure. He called his dad, but his Old Man didn't have any sympathy. He told him he'd just have to raise his game, so he did.

In his final year Andrew worked around the clock. Some nights he didn't sleep. Caffeine kept him going.

Andrew graduated in the top ten of his class and soon had his picks of jobs. He took a job at a major bank. His plan was to make a ton of money and retire early. That was the dream. But it wasn't just about the money – he wanted to make something of himself, to leave his mark on the world.

Andrew worked 15-hour days and prided himself on his ability to think clearly and logically in all situations. He went to the gym before work every morning – even if it meant getting up at 5:00 a.m. He drove himself hard. He could be a bit aggressive – but that was part of the game. He had no patience with people who didn't give 100 percent.

And when Andrew wasn't working hard, he played hard. He had a great group of guy friends and on the weekends when they weren't working they'd go camping and fishing or they'd fly off to exotic places to party.

By his late twenties, it was all going according to Andrew's plan except for one thing – his love life. He hadn't had a long-term relationship since he was at college. His

ex, Lucy, dumped him for being too possessive and cut-off emotionally – whatever the hell that meant. She'd been watching too much Oprah, if you asked him.

Andrew told himself that he was too busy to think about a relationship—and it's not like there was a short-age of women on his speed dial. He had to admit, though, that it was all starting to feel a bit empty.

Andrew is the classic example of the Masculine Strength Male, otherwise known as the Alpha Male. He's analytical, direct, intelligent, ambitious, and both mentally and physically strong. His focus and determi-nation bring him success everywhere in life—or almost everywhere.

But with the need to succeed comes a lot of pressure. From the youngest age, boys are told that they can't show weakness or vulnerability; they have to be tough and ag-gressive. This makes it hard for them to express their feelings, which in turn makes relationships hard.

Here are some of Andrew's traits:

Competitive

The main need of the Masculine Strength Male is to come out on top. Andrew says it himself: life is a competition and he wants to win. He wants to be the best at every-thing he does and he won't give up until he gets his goal.

Ambitious

Work is the priority of the Masculine Strength Male. It is where he gets his sense of purpose. While Feminine

Strength People go with the flow, Masculine Strength People are focused, driven and clear about what they want to do and how they will do it. They have five-year plans and will stop at nothing until they get there. Think of it as a throwback from the days when men hunted and kept their eye on their prey.

Confident

It never occurs to the Masculine Strength Male that he is wrong. He always says exactly what he thinks and he'll stick to his guns even when there's opposition. He's decisive, assertive and never doubts his abilities. People sense this confidence the moment he walks in the room—even if he doesn't say much. Actually, Masculine Strength Males often say very little. They know they don't need to.

Logical

The Masculine Strength Male thinks clearly, rationally and logically. He's a problem solver. He sees what needs to be done and does it. Emotions never get in his way. He stays calm in a crisis.

Successful

The main need of the Masculine Strength Male is to make something of himself in the world. While the feminine energy is all about introspection and feelings, the masculine energy is concerned with the outside world. He's often obsessed with success, status and wealth. It's not necessarily money itself that he wants – although the flashy house and car are nice. It's more that money is a marker of whether you're winning or not. Masculine Strength Males also feel an urgent need to leave their mark on the world, to fulfill their purpose. At the root of this is a need to feel good enough, to be acknowledged by the outside world. Feminine Strength People don't have this same need.

Strong
It's likely that most Masculine Strength Males have high testosterone levels. The male hormone creates a strong jawline and cheekbones, thicker brow ridges, larger noses, smaller eyes, thinner lips and a relatively long bottom half of the face. It also causes broader shoulders, strong upper arms and high muscle density. Andrew is a very strong man.

Loyal
The Masculine Strength Male is also very loyal. Once you're his friend, he will do anything for you. As a leader at work, he is loyal to his team. He'll show up and do what's needed – but he'll expect the same from the people around him. There's only one thing he won't do for his friends–talk for hours about their problems. He is practical, not emotional. He wants to fix problems, not moan about them.

In Control
It's important for the Masculine Strength Male to feel in control of his world, so he's disciplined, punctual and organized. He's the guy at the gym at 6:00 a.m. He

wants to know the quickest, most-efficient way to do everything.

Unexpressive

Despite appearances, the Masculine Strength Male does have struggles. While he can say what he thinks clearly and assertively, he finds it much harder to say what he feels. That's because half the time he doesn't really know what he feels. From the youngest age, many boys are brought up with the idea that real men don't have emotions. They're not allowed to cry, to be scared, or to be anxious. This has a hugely damaging effect on men— they learn early on to bottle up their emotions.

Judgmental

One of the main challenges that the Masculine Strength Male has is feeling empathy for others. Empathy is the ability to understand what others feel and to relate to that. Andrew doesn't have that ability. He's naturally confident and can't understand the insecurities of others. He doesn't have patience for anyone who can't move through life as easily as he does. At his worst, the Masculine Strength Male is arrogant, judgmental and thinks he's better than others.

Not Interested In Style

Unlike their Feminine Strength Friends, the Masculine Strength Male has no interest in aesthetics. However, he does realize that he has to dress well to get ahead, so he'll buy a quality wardrobe so that he doesn't need to think about it. Dressing well is a problem to be solved, not a form of self-expression.

Sleeps Around

We'll cover this more in the dating chapters, but the Masculine Strength Male is very likely to sleep around. Sex is his way to connect to the opposite sex. But he doesn't realize this, and it doesn't really work – he just finds himself getting one-night stands. There's no romance, no vulnerability, no intimacy—it's just sealing the deal. It's another conquest. This can be fun for a while, but eventually it starts to feel empty.

Can You Relate?

Do you relate to Andrew's story? Do you pride yourself on being clear-headed, ambitious and rational? Do you find it hard to empathize with others? When other people share their feelings do you think 'I don't know what you're talking about?" Do you get impatient and judgmental?

Remember that not all Masculine Strength Males will be the same. There is a spectrum of masculinity – just as there is a spectrum of femininity. You might fall on the extreme end, as Andrew does, or you could be more balanced.

And there will always be exceptions. I have another friend, Tom, who is also a Masculine Strength Male but who cannot relate to Andrew's lack of interest in conversations. He loves diving into discussions—even about emotions. But even though Tom likes to talk, he talks in a very masculine way. He's talking to get to the bottom of something, to solve a problem.

Once again I must stress that it's important to understand that we all have both masculine and feminine energy in us. You don't have just one or the other energy, you have both. It's just that for most of us one of these energies is more developed—whether through nature or conditioning. I know I keep repeating this, but it's very important to understand.

Remember that the purpose of this book is to balance your masculine and feminine energies so that you can draw on both energies equally and thus lead a full and healthy life.

SUMMARY

THE FOUR TYPES

IN THE LAST four chapters we examined the strengths and struggles of each of the four types of people.

We saw that Feminine Strength People are loving, creative, intuitive, empathetic and open. But they can also lose direction and spend more time pleasing others than themselves.

Masculine Strength People, on the other hand, get things done. They are motivated, disciplined, clear thinking and ambitious. There is nothing they cannot achieve easily—except love and connection. They find it hard to relax, to let go.

As we've seen, neither of the energies is better or worse. Both have amazing strengths but come with challenges.

The question I put to you now is what if you could learn to be the best of both worlds? What if you could be strong and direct like Chloe and Andrew, while also being caring, fun and intuitive, like Lily and Chris?

What if you could still be spontaneous and creative as

a Feminine Strength Person, yet you could also embrace discipline, structure and action? What if you could actually bring your many ideas to life? How would your life be transformed if you learned to create boundaries and care for yourself while also being able to care for others?

Or, for the Masculine Strength Person, wouldn't it be great if you could keep all your drive and ambition, but also be able to relax, sit still, and feel at peace? How would your life change if you could be logical and focused but also tap into your creativity and intuition? And wouldn't it be wonderful to use your heart as well as your head? To really love others as well as yourself?

Well, all this is possible. You CAN be the best of both worlds. You CAN be a perfect blend of the masculine and feminine energy.

This is what The Bingo Theory is about.

In the following chapters you'll find out just how to become a Bingo, with simple, practical tips. I promise it will change your life.

III

PART THREE

Bingo

.....

"We are not meant to be perfect. We are meant to be whole."

— JANE FONDA

8

BINGO! THE WINNING COMBINATION

I RECENTLY WATCHED a new version of the classic fairytale – Cinderella, on a flight back from New York. Most of us know the story of the poor country girl who is left in the care of a wicked stepmother and ugly stepsisters. But in this version there was a line in it that I had not noticed before.

Just before she dies, Cinderella's mother leans forward and says to her daughter: "I want to tell you a secret that will see you through all the trials that life can offer. You must always remember this. *Have courage and be kind. Have courage and be kind, my darling.*"

Cinderella takes this advice to heart. Throughout the film we see her being kind to everyone around her. She is kind to her stepmother, even though she's vicious. She is kind to her stepsisters, even though they're bullies. But kindness alone is not enough.

One day while she is out in the forest, escaping her mean stepsisters, Cinderella gets caught up in a hunt. Men from the palace are hunting a beautiful stag. Cinderella's kindness makes it impossible for her to watch such cruelty, and so she stands up to the Prince and says, "What has this deer done to you? You're frightening the life out of him. Please don't hurt him."

The Prince falls in love with her in that moment – the moment she is both courageous and kind.

As the story progresses, Cinderella goes to the ball and the Prince falls in love with her all over again. But her wicked stepmother tries to ruin the romance by locking Cinderella in the attic. Yet again, Cinderella is called upon to be courageous again. She stands up to her stepmother and tells her that she will never do as she says. Only then does she find happiness and love. The Prince finds her in the attic, and they live happily ever after.

When I watched that movie I was stunned. It struck me that kindness and courage are completely different things. Kindness comes from our feminine energy. Courage comes from the masculine.

Cinderella was taught from the earliest age that she needed to draw on both the masculine and the feminine energies. It's not enough to just be kind; people will walk all over you. It's also not enough to just be courageous. Courage can turn into aggression and violence, as it did with the Prince's mindless hunting.

"Oh my God," I thought. "Cinderella is a Bingo!"

A Bingo is when you balance your masculine and feminine energies. You are kind *and* courageous. Confident *and* caring. The power and magic lie in being both—and in knowing when to use the right energy at the right time.

This is the ultimate message of this book.

The Perfect 10

The people we admire on a global scale have a balance of both energies. People such as Martin Luther King or Mother Theresa, Oprah Winfrey or Bill Clinton are caring yet strong, creative yet decisive, vulnerable yet powerful. They followed their hearts and took action, even in the face of great danger. They were single-minded and yet driven by the greater good.

And if you were to describe your dream partner, how would you do it?

Guys often rate women when they meet them. A woman is a ten when she has a great body, long hair, beautiful eyes, nice skin—and when she has a strong and confident personality. She's sensual and sexy, and yet she isn't afraid to get her hands dirty and change a punctured wheel.

If you ask a lot of women what they want in a man, they'll say they want a man who is powerful and successful but also sweet, romantic and caring. He's a financial provider but he's also there for the children. He's an animal in bed but will also be a domestic God and help with the cooking and cleaning.

Again, these are two completely different qualities. Most guys who earn the big bucks are not the guys who make it home in time to cook you dinner.

And most women who lure you in with their feminine charms are not the women who you'll find under a car bonnet.

These are combinations of masculine and feminine energies. At the end of the day, everybody's looking for a Bingo.

Soon I will show you how to find that. But this book

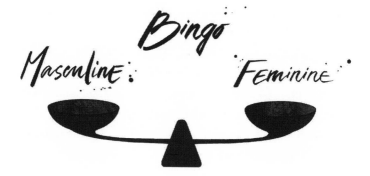

isn't just about finding a partner. It's about learning to be the best you that you can be, so that you can thrive in work, in life *and* in love.

The secret is that we have to accept and express both our masculine and feminine energies in order to live a full, productive, happy life. This is also our greatest challenge.

According to Joseph Campbell, the author of a number of famous books on comparative mythology, the hero of any story is always someone who uses both their masculine and feminine energy. In many myths the hero is even the offspring of the sun god (masculine energy) and the moon goddess (feminine energy). It's his ability to draw on both the masculine energies of logic and courage and the feminine energies of caring and intuition that make him able to save the day when nobody else can.

When we learn to do the same, we too can be heroes.

Leonardo Da Vinci was a Bingo

Did you know that Leonardo Da Vinci was a Bingo? He was a genius in both science (masculine) and art (feminine) and he was dedicated to both logic (masculine) and beauty (feminine). It's believed that his left and right brain hemispheres were extremely well connected and this allowed him to think both logically and creatively.

Art experts argue that his portraits – most notable of which is the Mona Lisa – are so appealing because they contain the dual characteristics of masculine and feminine. Da Vinci, himself has even been described as being "somewhere between the masculine and the feminine."

It's been suggested that Albert Einstein also had high

levels of connectivity between each hemisphere, allowing him to engage in "whole brain thinking."

Research has shown that people who are leaders in their fields often display a balance of masculine and feminine energies. In a fascinating book— *Creativity: Flow and the Psychology of Discovery and Invention*, psychologist Mihaly Csikszentmihalyi observes that the world's greatest creative talents tend to be psychologically androgynous.

Csikszentmihalyi explains that throughout time, men have been raised to be 'masculine' while women have been raised to be 'feminine'. Creative people, however, seem to be the exception to this stereotyping. When tested as children, creative girls tend to be "more dominant and tough than other girls" while "creative boys are more sensitive and less aggressive than their male peers."

Csikszentmihalyi argues that this is a winning combination. Women artists and scientists use their masculine energy to get their work noticed, while creative men use their feminine energy to make them highly sensitive to the world and to relationships.

What you will gain by learning about you energies

While I cannot promise you that you will become the next Leonardo Da Vinci or Einstein, here's what you will learn in the next few chapters.

If you are a Feminine Strength Person you will learn how to:

- Take charge of your life, your career and your finances.
- Stand up for yourself and articulate yourself calmly

and directly.
- Plan ahead, set goals and actually make your plans happen.
- Replace feelings of fear with power; swap lethargy for energy.

The natural feminine qualities of empathy, creativity, love and intuition can be combined with the masculine qualities of action, focus, determination and confidence. And I will teach you how to achieve this winning combination.

If you are a Masculine Strength Person you will learn how to:

- Get in touch with your emotions. Yes, you do have them, despite what you might think. And no, embracing your emotions will not make you weak.
- Become more empathetic and connect with others by opening your heart.
- Rest, sit still and relax. And this is not a sign of weakness, it's a vital part of life – a time to re-charge and renew. A time when great ideas can come your way.
- Let go and trust. You can't control everything as much as you'd like to think you can. It's when you let go and trust, that things happen as they are meant to happen.

The masculine qualities of clear-thinking, ambition, courage and action can be combined with the softer feminine qualities of love, connection and creativity. And this book will teach you how to achieve this winning combination.

And What About Relationships?

Later in the book, we will address what this means in terms of your relationships. For now, the important thing is to focus on yourself. Be assured, however, that once you are a Bingo, everything transforms. After all, Cinderella found her prince didn't she? When you are a Bingo people will be drawn to you like a magnet because everybody wants to be around the perfect combination of masculine and feminine energies. And for those of you who are already in a relationship, learning to be a Bingo will enable you to have a happier, healthier relationship with your partner.

But Why Do We Need to Balance?

You might wonder why it is so important to be a balance of both masculine and feminine energies. Why don't we just play to our strengths?

For example, if you're a Masculine Strength Person who is decisive and ambitious, why don't you just build on those skills? And if you're a Feminine Strength Person who is kind and caring, why do you need to be ambitious or organized?

That's certainly the approach most people take in life—they play to their strengths. Unfortunately it doesn't work.

Our strengths are our strengths only when they are used in moderation—without balance they become destructive.

Consider Yin and Yang again. Yin is water, Yang is

sun. The Yang's sun is a powerful source of energy and it gives us life. But without Yin's water there would be drought and everything would die.

But how does this imbalance become destructive in real life?

Too Much Feminine = Depressed

To explain how an imbalance of energies can be destructive let's catch up with Lily, our Feminine Strength Female and Chris, our Feminine Strength Male, to see what happened when they relied solely on their feminine energy.

Let's start with Lily, who was drifting along at the interior design magazine where she'd worked for the past five years:

Lily's magazine folded. She got a good pay off, which meant she didn't have to rush to get another job, so she decided to take a bit of time off.

It was great at first – a dream life. She slept in, went to yoga and met friends for dinner. She didn't keep tabs on how much she was spending, though. She wanted to enjoy the here and now.

Soon she was enjoying the 'now' a bit too much. Without work to get up for, a quiet dinner with friends somehow turned into an all-nighter. She was drinking a lot and sometimes taking drugs too. At night she had fun but the next day she'd feel depressed. Soon she went to the other extreme and stopped going out.

Lily knew she needed to start applying for jobs but she kept putting it off. As the months passed, she start-

ed to feel scared of going back into the working world. She signed up for self-development courses instead. She also read a lot about spirituality – shamanism was her current obsession. It was all very interesting but she was losing her grip on reality.

Some days she felt like she was drowning. She had too much time to think. She felt lost and alone. She began to cry most days and eat too much. She knew she needed to pull herself together and do something, but she never managed to.

When Feminine Strength People rely on their feminine energy alone a couple of things can happen. First they can become hedonistic, party people. After all, they are living in the moment, having fun, connecting! All this sounds great. But without proper structure such people get lost in their feelings and lose their grip on the outside world.

Then they go to the other extreme and become entirely introverted. They become paralyzed because they lack the masculine energy that drives action and structure. They stop *doing* and get stuck just *being*. Slowly this turns into isolation and depression.

They may be prone to eating and drinking their way through their feelings. Cookies-and-ice cream and red wine were all invented for Feminine Strength People in a major slump – as were self-help books.

Too much feminine energy causes you to be passive and to look to others for leadership. However, endlessly reading books about astrology, shamanism and the law of attraction won't pay your credit card bills. Self-help books are great if you actually *do* what they suggest; otherwise, they are another form of procrastination.

The extreme feminine energy can manifest in other ways as well.

Let's catch up with Chris, our Feminine Strength Male, who also relied too heavily on his feminine energy.

After five years of talking about leaving his graphic design job to start his own business, Chris finally took the plunge. He had a great idea for a new dating site and when his grandmother died, leaving him some inheritance, he decided to seize the day and quit his job.

He was excited at first. He got flashy business cards made and bought a new laptop. He didn't have a business plan as such; he was just going to wing it. He had the idea and the enthusiasm – that was enough, right?

A couple of months in, reality started to hit. First of all, he couldn't decide on the name for the site. Everyone had different opinions and he couldn't figure out which was best. Plus, working with the development team was a nightmare – they kept asking for direction and he didn't know what to tell them. He felt overwhelmed by choices. He didn't know what the right thing to do was – he wanted someone else to tell him.

After a year working on his site it still wasn't live and his money had run out. He couldn't afford his rent so he gave up his apartment and moved home. His father laughed at him. He told him it was time to stop dreaming and come back to the family tiling business to earn some money. He felt humiliated. So much for the big dream – he was now working for the family business, listening to his dad lecture him on what a loser he was.

In Chris's case, relying only on his feminine energy resulted in a failed business. Chris had a great idea but he didn't have the confidence, energy or focus (which come from our masculine energy) to make it into a reality. He couldn't make decisions and soon got overwhelmed.

Feminine Strength People want someone else to take charge. This can be a problem when you're the boss. They constantly look for reassurance and think that other people's opinions of them are right. When Chris's dad doubted him, Chris believed his dad's view and gave up too quickly. Feminine Strength People can be quick to go into 'Poor Me' victim mode and find it hard to stand up for themselves.

Too Much Feminine Energy Can Cause You to Be:

Lethargic
Depressed
Overweight
Overwhelmed
Confused
Isolated
Passive

Too Much Masculine Energy = Burnout

So what happens on the other end of the spectrum—when you let only your masculine energy run the show?

Remember Chloe? Our Masculine Strength Female from a few chapters back? Here's what happened to her when she worked solely from her masculine energy.

After 8 years of working 15-hour days in her law practice, Chloe was getting close to being made a junior partner. All the hard work was paying off. But it didn't make her any happier.

The truth was she had become perpetually angry and bitter. Most days, she found herself shouting at people in the office, even making one of the assistants cry. But for God's sake, she thought, why can't these girls have some backbone? What's wrong with everyone? Does nobody else care about doing a good job? It was fine for the men, who all hang out in their old boy's network, but she had to be tougher if she was going to hold her own.

And it wasn't like she had someone at home looking after her, the way they do. Her personal life was non-existent. Sometimes she went on dates but none of the guys were clever enough for her. All her friends were busy in the suburbs with their husbands and children. She told herself that she didn't want what they had but she didn't know if that was true.

Chloe spent her thirtieth birthday alone in the office, working late.

She had birthday plans with her parents but they cancelled—they were also working. Once again she got the message that she was not as important as their careers.

That night, on her ride back to her empty apartment she found herself looking into bars and restaurants with people smiling and laughing and talking with friends. She couldn't remember the last time she had done that. She couldn't remember the last time she had left the office before midnight. She was lonely. Very, very lonely.

Using her masculine energy worked for Chloe in many ways. She was on her way to becoming one of the youngest partners at her law firm and she had great financial success. But it came at a price.

Chloe had always been a kind and loyal person, but over the years she had become angry and bitter. She was impatient with colleagues and pushed away the people who loved her by always putting work first.

Chloe never allowed herself time to stop and look at the big picture. She never asked herself the big questions like whether or not she wanted to start a family, or what she really wanted from life. Those things were too uncomfortable to think about and so she did what she always did—she pushed down her feelings of loneliness and focused on the next rung of the ladder.

Andrew, our Masculine Strength Male, had a very similar but more intense experience. He was working round the clock at the bank, and like Chloe he was very successful – on paper at least.

When Andrew turned thirty, he knew he was at a crossroad. He could either keep doing what he was doing –working hard, playing hard and sleeping around – or he could settle down, as some of his friends were.

He chose to keep doing what he was doing. After all,

he was living the dream, right? In fact, he decided to put more hours in at work and set the insane target of doubling his bonus next year.

For the next two years, Andrew worked 24/7. He flew around the world in business class and signed major deals. He was the young hot shot. He bought expensive cars, a high-class apartment and had the best of everything.

He was developing a reputation for being brutal at work but he didn't care – he did what needed to be done. He didn't have time to worry about other people's feelings – if they couldn't take it, they should not be there.

He also didn't have time for a relationship – or at least that's what he told himself – so he kept himself to one-night stands. They were almost too easy to find. He was a good-looking guy with a lot of money – he could pick women up anywhere. Soon he started to despise the girls he was with – he had no respect for them. Although, to be honest, he didn't have respect for many people anymore. Andrew's arrogance has become extreme. Everything around him pointed to the fact that he was simply better than everyone else.

But Andrew's hyper pace of lifestyle began to take its toll. After a couple of years he began to have problems sleeping. He found it hard to focus at work and couldn't think straight. He started forgetting things. He had a hard time getting up in the morning.

Then, one day he had a panic attack on a flight. He couldn't understand why – he'd been on hundreds of flights. What was happening?

Both Chloe and Andrew decided it was easier to use their masculine energy, rather than work on their feminine energy. And in a lot of ways that worked for them – they were incredibly productive and successful. But they also led very empty lives.

When Masculine Strength People rely only on their masculine energy, they go after external goals or achievements irrespective of anything else. They go after money and status.

The result is that they burn out. We need our feminine energy in order to love and care for ourselves and for others. Without it, Masculine Strength People can self-destruct.

They also tend to cut themselves off from people. Because they are cut off from their heart and feelings they become cold, insensitive and emotionally closed off, reckless, overly-critical and aggressive. In fact, when it's not balanced with feminine energy, the masculine energy is often connected with heart problems.

Too Much Masculine Energy Can Cause You to Be:

Cold

Judgmental

Impatient

At risk of burnout

Greedy

Aggressive

Violent

Controlling

Cynical

Angry

Overly materialistic

So having looked at these four examples, we can see it doesn't work to just play to our strengths. If we do that our strengths can destroy us.

When Masculine Strength People don't use their feminine energy they become disconnected from their feelings. They don't know how to love themselves or others. They can become angry, aggressive and obsessed with work. They're unable to find peace.

Without using their masculine energy, Feminine Strength People don't know how to stand up for themselves and make their way through the world. They can be paralyzed by fear and lost in their feelings.

We need both energies in order to have a fulfilled life. We need action and stillness, thinking and feeling, outward focus and inward focus.

Let's return to the fairy tale. If Cinderella relied solely on her kindness she would still be locked up in the attic with her wicked stepmother. If the Prince hadn't learned to be kind, he'd be out hunting animals by day and partying by night, slowly turning into a cold, aggressive, heartless man. And that's not a happy ending, is it?

We need to use both the masculine and feminine energy in our lives– and the good news is we have both. It's just that one has become more developed in us through either nature or conditioning. The purpose of this book is to teach you how to balance your masculine and feminine energies so that you can use both equally and live a full and happy life; so that you can become your own hero or heroine.

How do we do that? Read on.

9

CHAPTER IX

BECOMING A BINGO
FOR FEMININE STRENGTH
MEN AND WOMEN

IN THIS CHAPTER, we'll discover how Feminine Strength Females and Males can bring out their masculine energy. I'll share simple, actionable steps that you can take right away. If you're a Masculine Strength Female or Male, feel free to move on to the next chapter, where you'll learn how to bring out your feminine energy.

How do we balance our energies? How do we become a Bingo?

The first step is to Own Your Strength.

If you are a Feminine Strength Person, like Lily or Chris, you are probably kind, caring, connected, intuitive and creative. You're popular and easy going. You have many wonderful qualities as a result of this strength—but you don't need to develop them anymore. Instead you need to bring out your organized, confident, go-getting masculine energy.

How do you do that?

Let me show you how Lily brought out her masculine energy.

Remember that Lily lost all structure in her life after she was laid off from her job; she started partying and living off credit cards. Then she became isolated and depressed. How did she come out of her situation?

The best thing that happened to Lily was that her money ran out.

Lily thought the money would last forever, but it didn't. In fact, she burnt through it within a year. Then her credit card debt began mounting. She asked her parents for a loan but for the first time ever they refused. "It's time to stand up on your own two feet," her mother told her. "We've been helping you out long enough."

Lily was outraged, but it was the shock she needed to wake up. She contacted everyone she knew, looking for work. A friend told her about a job that was much more senior to the one she had had at the magazine.

It was the role of deputy editor at a design website and it involved managing people and budgets – something she had no experience with – but out of desperation, she applied. To her utter amazement the interview went well and she got offered the job.

For the first two months, she felt out of her league. The job stretched her in every way. She had to be organized and responsible, show leadership and manage the books. But she amazed herself by doing it. She had a few tough moments – mostly when she had to confront staff about poor work – but she learned to handle those conversations. She could see that people respected her for making a stand.

The boost to her confidence was so strong that she felt like she could do anything. Her energy went through the roof – so much so that she joined the gym at work and started doing high- intensity workouts. The lethargy was gone. She stopped drinking during the week. She was able to think clearly for the first time in years. She felt that anything was possible.

Lily was forced by her financial conditions to develop her masculine energy. Challenging situations can often be our greatest teachers.

She could have continued living off credit cards, but she didn't. Instead, she used her masculine energy to get real and take action. She didn't think she was good enough for the job but she went for it anyway—again, this was her masculine energy.

Feminine Strength People doubt their abilities while Masculine Strength People think they can rule the world. Somewhere in between 'poor me, I'm useless' and 'check me out, I'm fabulous' is a great place to be.

For people like Lily it is sometimes necessary to fake it till you make it. When she got the job she had to fake it. She had to take on organization, leadership and management. None of this came easily to her but she did it.

Lily also had to face one of her greatest fears – confrontation. She still felt shaken up after such conversations, but she learned how to hold her own. The ability to hold your own makes a huge impact in all areas of life. If you can learn to stand up for yourself at work you will find it easier to do it in your personal life as well.

Vigorous exercise also really helped Lily. She ditched her yoga class, with its plinky-plonky music, and toughed it out in the gym, lifting weights and breaking a sweat. As she got physically strong, she got mentally strong.

As a result of working out, Lily started to feel more powerful, more in control.

Meanwhile, Chris, our Feminine Strength Male developed his masculine energy in a different way.

Working for his domineering dad made Chris miserable. For months he sat in the family office listening to his father make belittling remarks about how Chris would never amount to anything; how Chris should have saved himself a lot of time and come straight to the family firm.

One day Chris snapped. "I am done," he said, "I'd rather starve than spend another minute listening to you." Chris walked out of the family business that day and he never went back. His heart raced as he walked away – it was the first time he stood up to his father like that.

That night Chris asked a friend if he could crash on his sofa for a while, while he sorted things out. He got in touch with his old boss and she offered him freelance shifts. In the evenings he worked on his dating site—enough messing around. This time he was going to make this happen.

For weeks he felt like he was getting nowhere. He couldn't afford proper developers, so he taught himself the tech side. It was slow process but he kept at it. Then, one day, he bumped into a guy he went to school with.

They didn't know each other well but they had a coffee and it turned out Harry was a developer.

Harry didn't pull any punches. 'This site is a mess,' he said, looking at the beginnings of the dating site. The old Chris would have run away but the new Chris knew he had to take the criticism.

Harry sent him away with a bunch of tasks and told him to get back to him by the end of the month. Chris did what Harry recommended and Harry gave him more recommendations. Again, Chris followed through.

After a few months, Harry suggested they go into business together. They were the perfect match – Harry (a Masculine Strength Male) was experienced and solid. Chris was creative and had great contacts. It was the beginning of great things.

The moment Chris stood up to his father was the moment he started using his masculine energy. Feminine Strength people can tolerate abuse in a way that Masculine Strength People would never accept. Feminine Strength People value other people's opinions over their own, and as a result of this they can become dangerously passive. They can become victims. They need to use their masculine energy to stand up for themselves.

Chris also used his masculine energy when he took financial responsibility. He walked away from the security of his father's business and family home and stood on his own two feet. Feminine Strength People can be too quick to rely on others. There's a power that comes from looking after yourself.

Next, Chris did another thing he had never done before – he used his masculine energy to work consistently and with focus. He was smart enough to know that he needed someone to help him be accountable, someone to give him a plan and a list of goals.

What's more is that Chris followed through. For months he did exactly what he said he would do—a trait that does not come easily to the flaky feminine energy. This proved to Harry that he was a worthy business partner.

How to Develop Your Masculine Energy

Not all of us go to the extremes that Lily and Chris did, but if you are a Feminine Strength Person, here are some strategies for you to use to bring out your masculine energy. These tips apply to both Feminine Strength Males and Females.

Don't think you need to do all of them at once. Pick one or two things that you can do this week. It is better to make small but consistent baby steps than to do too much and then give up after a month.

Have a Plan

This is the single-most important thing you need to do. Really! While the Masculine Strength People draw up their five year plans the Feminine Strength People don't even know what they're doing that evening. Being spontaneous is great, but without a plan in life you will feel lost and aimless. A good plan acts like a map. It gives you direction and focus – both of which give your masculine energy a boost. As Benjamin Franklin said: "If you fail to plan, you plan to fail."

There are a million ways to plan, but here are a few ideas:

- **YOUR LIFE PLAN:** Block off an afternoon to decide what it is you would like to achieve in your life. An activity that may help is to cut out pictures and create a vision board. For more information you can watch my video on Youtube - How to Make Your Dreams Come True. Review your plan regularly. It will change as you do – and that's fine. Nothing is set in stone. This is just a way of getting clarity on your life.

- **ANNUAL PLAN:** Write down ten things you want to achieve this year. Now, break them down into months. What can you do when? Be realistic and specific with your deadlines. Put them in your calendar.

- **WEEKLY PLAN:** Every Sunday afternoon or evening set goals for the week ahead. Again, give yourself specific deadlines. Thinking that you will do something in the next couple of weeks isn't good enough. Schedule all your tasks into your calendar. If it doesn't get scheduled, it doesn't get done.

- **DAILY PLAN:** Ten minutes of planning every morning will transform your day. Begin every morning by asking yourself "What is the most important thing I need to do today?" Get that done first. I love a product called the Productivity Planner, which helps to plan your day by breaking it down into half hour segments. This is a product that I have co-created with my business partners Alex and UJ to make our lives easier and more productive.

All of this might sound like a lot of work, but I promise

that it will make you feel much more grounded and in control. Feminine Strength People like to say that they are free-spirited and fun – which they are – but the reality is that they often spend their lives feeling overwhelmed and stressed. Planning eliminates a lot of that stress.

When you focus on what you have to accomplish, you become less focused on your ever-changing emotions and life become simpler. You know when to work and what to do and it gives you the satisfaction of crossing off achievements. To quote Phil Copeland, "The trouble with not having a goal is that you spend your life running up and down the field and you never score." It's time to start scoring.

Accountability

Research shows you are much more likely to achieve your goals if you are accountable to someone else. Find a coach or a no-nonsense friend who will check up on you. Tell them what you plan to do and by when. Make sure they are a Masculine Strength Person who won't take any excuses.

Vigorous Exercise

After planning, vigorous exercise is the most life-changing thing that Feminine Strength People can do—and no, I don't mean walking around the block or doing a nice bit of yoga. I mean proper, hard-core exercise. Studies show that high-intensity workouts, including heavy weights and body weight, boost testosterone production and give you a rush of endorphins – which will give you a rush of the masculine energy. Boxing and martial arts are also a great way to feel stronger and more powerful. Team events such as boot camps are good because they make you accountable. Sign up to a class now. Put it in your calendar. Commit, commit, commit!

Power Pose

Recent research shows that if you strike a powerful pose – where you take up as much space as possible – your testosterone (masculine hormone) levels increase and your cortisol (stress hormone) levels decrease. Feminine Strength People are prone to fear and self-doubt. If you want to feel a rush of masculine confidence, simply lift your chin, put your shoulders back and open up your body. This makes you look – and feel – more assertive. Before a big meeting, stand for two minutes in the 'wonder woman' pose, with your legs wide and your hands on your waist. It's amazing how much stronger it makes you feel.

Spend Time with Masculine Strength People

Motivational speaker Jim Rohn famously said that we are the average of the five people we spend the most time with. So who do you spend time with? Do you hang out with other Feminine Strength People? If so, it's time to make new friends. Spending time with Masculine Strength People will help bring out your masculine energy. You might not feel like you have a lot in common at first, but you will both learn from each other. My feminine energy friends always tell me that they feel clearer, stronger and more confident after we spend time together.

Meditate

Meditation helps clear your mind, keep you focused and stay calm—much needed skills for Feminine Strength People. The more you do it, the greater control you will have over your emotions. You will no longer be hostage to them. However, to get the benefits of meditation, you need to stick to it –this means using your masculine energy to be consistent and disciplined. Start small, with ten minutes of meditation every morning and evening. You can make the sessions longer as you get more practice.

Take on Challenges

Take on big work projects, agree to do public speaking, ask for a pay rise. It doesn't matter what it is, and it doesn't matter if you succeed. All that matters is that you aim high and take action. Masculine Strength People love a challenge, so take one and it will bring out your masculine energy.

Be Honest

Ask a Masculine Strength Person if your bum looks big, and they'll tell you the truth. Ask a Feminine Strength Person and they'll tell you that you look beautiful even if what you are wearing isn't flattering. Feminine Strength People are endlessly polite and diplomatic. They don't say what they really think for fear of hurting other people. They also don't stand up for themselves or ask for what they want because they fear the other person's reaction. To bring out your masculine energy, be direct and honest in your communication. Say what you mean and ask for what you need. Be assertive. People are not mind readers, and while others might not like what you say, they will always respect you when you speak the truth.

Keep Your Word

Feminine Strength People can be unreliable. They have the best of intentions but they make all sorts of promises that they don't follow through on. They cancel at the last minute and fail to meet deadlines. They make excuses. Does this sound like you? Be honest. This habit annoys other people and it disempowers you. It makes you think you can't do anything you say you'll do. When you follow through on something even when you don't want to do it, you will feel a surge of personal power. For one week make it a goal to do everything you say you will do, even if you don't feel like it. You will be amazed at how much stronger this makes you feel.

Eat More Protein

Feminine Strength People are prone to emotional highs and lows. The last thing you need to add to that is sugar highs and lows. To feel strong and calm, eat a clean, healthy diet that is rich in vegetables and protein. Protein is necessary to build lean muscles and it gives you sustained energy throughout the day. Eat at least a palm-sized amount of protein with your meals, and snack on seeds and nuts, or nut butters. Good sources of protein include quinoa, beans, lentils, spirulina, nuts and seeds.

Power Dress

Experiments have shown that not only do our clothes affect how other people view us, they also affect how we feel, think, and act. For example, volunteers wearing a doctor's coat performed better in tasks that required close attention than those wearing normal clothes. Other studies have shown that people perform better in negotiations when wearing a suit, compared to when they are in jeans and a t-shirt. Our clothes convey messages of status, power and self-worth. Therefore, if you want to feel more powerful, start power dressing. Sharp-tailoring and darker colors will bring out your masculine energy.

Puzzles

Take on mental challenges with mind teasers and crossword puzzles. Read serious non-fiction such as business books or anything that will bring out your logical, fact-driven masculine energy. Fiction helps Masculine Strength People get in touch with feelings and creativity, but this comes easily to Feminine Strength People. What you need to do is become more rational; a better problem solver. They say that information is power. Inform yourself about history, business, or science and this will help you focus on the outside world instead of the inner world of feelings.

Volunteer

Help out in the local homeless shelter, teach in a third world country or volunteer with children. Feminine Strength People are caring and can cry over all the atrocities they see on the news. They *feel* other people's pain acutely. But they rarely tend to *do* much about it. Doing something to help another person takes you out of yourself. People live in circumstances you can't even imagine. When you engage in physically doing something about it, you will feel grounded, strong and empowered.

Get Your Hands Dirty

Go camping, take up gardening, learn to change a tire. Do anything that gets your hands dirty – literally. Feminine Strength People like the luxuries in life and don't like muck or mess. Getting your hands dirty will bring out your masculine energy. Here's a crazy statistic: men who chop wood experience a 46.8 percent increase in their testosterone levels. Maybe it's time to do more than just wear that lumberjack shirt!

DIY

Can you change a light-bulb, put up a shelf, or assemble a piece of furniture? If you can't, then learn how. Feminine Strength People will happily wait around for someone else to do practical jobs for them. Doing it yourself will make you feel powerful, confident and in control of your life. Big claims for a little light-bulb, but try it.

Make a Decision

Feminine Strength People can spend twenty minutes looking at a menu and then ask their dining companion to order for them. They lack the confidence to make choices; they drown in options, so practice making decisions. Start small. Decide quickly on what you want to eat in a restaurant. Make a decision about something you have been procrastinating about at work. Accept the fact that once you make a decision it's done. Don't over-analyze or worry about the results. It's OK to make mistakes, they help you grow and learn. The fact is that once Feminine Strength People get the confidence to make decisions they, usually make the right ones, thanks to their great intuition.

Cut Up The Credit Cards

Last but not least, get rid of your credit cards. Now. Please. The tendencies that Feminine Strength People have to enjoy beautiful things and live-for-the moment are lethal when combined with a credit card. Remove all temptation. Masculine Strength People can be organized with their money. They keep track of it and they want more of it. Follow their lead and make it a habit to check your bank balances every day. If you are in debt, that's OK. Don't beat yourself up about it or play the victim. Facing the facts is the first step. Now, make a plan to earn more money, or to manage the money you have more effectively. Get busy selling stuff on eBay, ask for a pay raise, stop buying scented candles...get real with your finances.

"Educating the mind, without educating the heart is no education at all"

— ARISTOTLE

10

BECOMING A BINGO
FOR MASCULINE STRENGTH
MEN AND WOMEN

IN THIS CHAPTER we'll discover how Masculine Strength Females and Males can bring out their feminine energy. I'll share simple, actionable tips that you can practice right away.

The first step is to Own Your Strength.

As a Masculine Strength Person, you're strong, ambitious, reliable and confident. You're probably flying high at work, and have your finances in order, so most likely you don't need to work on that side of yourself any more. You do not need to spend more time in the office – do you hear that?

Instead you need to slow down and open up; connect with yourself and with others. You need to get in touch with those weird things called 'feelings'.

How do you do that?

Let me show you how my friend Chloe brought out her feminine energy. You may remember that Chloe was on the verge of being made the youngest partner at her law firm after years of hard work and sacrifice. She spent her 30th birthday alone in the office, but she told herself it was all for a greater cause.

Shortly after her solitary birthday, Chloe was called into a meeting where she was told she wasn't going to make partner. "The timing's not right, maybe next year," the other partners told her.

She felt like she had been kicked in the stomach. She felt betrayed. She felt her world crumble.

For the next six months Chloe kept going to work but for the first time in her life, she didn't care. She did the bare minimum. She could hardly look her colleagues in the eye. She felt like they were all laughing at her.

At night she went home and sat in front of the television. Weekends stretched out endlessly. She didn't know what to do with herself. She realized how empty her life was outside of work.

Then one day she called her old school friend, Anna. "I don't know what I'm doing with my life," she said. "For the first time in my life, I don't know what's next. I don't have a plan." She cried for the first time in as long as she could remember—and it felt good.

Over the next few months Chloe met up with old friends. She went to visit them and meet their children. She used to look down on these people for leading boring, ordinary lives. But now they seemed like the lucky ones. They had love and people around them. What did Chloe have? Slowly but surely Chloe realized that if she wanted to get a life, she needed to get away from work.

She went to HR and did something unthinkable – she asked for a three- month sabbatical.

A set back at work can cause Masculine Strength People to reassess their whole lives. This is usually a good thing. For years Chloe got her sense of identity and purpose from her work. It wasn't just one part of her life – it was her whole life.

When Chloe got passed up for the partnership, it was devastating. She felt humiliated, let down, like a failure. But it was a good lesson to her that although work is important it should never be a person's whole life. That cliché came to life for her: nobody lies on their death bed wishing they'd spent more time in the office. Friendships, relationships and love are what really matter – and to access those you need to use your feminine energy.

Chloe started reaching out to old friends and for the first time in her life she was vulnerable with them. Instead of being the one with all the answers, she admitted she was struggling. Instead of being the one to help everyone else, she let others help her. All of this involved using her feminine energy.

The amazing thing was that this did not make her feel weak- quite the opposite. She felt the power of being loved. She realized that she didn't need to 'do' anything, she could just 'be'. Sometimes that was enough. For once she felt at peace.

Now, what about Andrew, our Masculine Strength Male who was on the brink of burning out? He wasn't able to sleep and it was affecting his work. It felt like his mind—the mind that had gotten him so far— was spinning out of control.

Andrew had not slept properly in weeks, and was finding it impossible to concentrate. His bosses were noticing. He became constantly fearful of when the next panic attack would come – what if it happened in the middle of a meeting? His mind was racing all the time. He couldn't switch off. In the middle of the night, he'd Google things like: 'I can't focus. I am having a hard time going to work. My mind is all over the place. What is depression?'

Finally, Andrew reached out to John, an old family friend, who was in town for a couple of nights. Over dinner, he told John everything. It was the first time he'd admitted to anyone what was happening.

John listened patiently until Andrew had run out of words.

"This is your body's way of telling you it's time to slow down," John said. "You're not losing it – actually it's quite the opposite. This is your wake up call."

He asked Andrew a series of questions: Where do you want to be ten years from now? Not professionally, but personally. What kind of a man do you want to be? Do you want to keep going down the path you are on? Do you want to be the kind of man that sleeps with twenty-year-olds when he's fifty? Don't you want more in your life than work?

Andrew responded that he planned to retire at forty-five – once he'd made his millions. He just needed to keep focused for the next few years.

"If you keep going the way you're going, you'll have

a heart attack by the time you're forty-five," said John. "I've seen it happen."

It was a shock.

Shortly after that dinner, Andrew bumped into his ex-girlfriend, from college. They were at a mutual friend's wedding. She was there with her husband and their baby. She looked beautiful and happy. He felt that same feeling he had when they were together all those years ago –she was everything he was not.

The next day he went to the doctor and got signed off from work for two months due to stress.

For the first two weeks, he didn't leave the house. He slept, he watched television, he looked at the ceiling. Then a book arrived in the post. It was from John, and it was called —the Power of Now. He didn't understand it entirely, but he read a bit every night. He started meditating ten minutes a day and it seemed to help. He even went away on a meditation retreat. It was torture to sit still and face the nothingness of life – but he did it and it helped him tremendously to feel calm, peaceful and equanimous.

One weekend he went back to his parents' house. It was his first visit in months. He slept in his childhood room and walked around the park he used to play in as a child. He found his old guitar and picked it up. He started playing around with it. He wasn't any good but it didn't matter. Playing it relaxed him. Slowly but surely he started to feel calmer. He felt like he had come back home, in more ways than one.

It is very easy for Masculine Strength People to work

crazy hours and burn out. Work, after all, is everything to them. They ignore the signs that they need to slow down until they get sick, stop sleeping or get panic attacks, as Andrew did.

Andrew was terrified of admitting any weakness to others and of asking for help, but reaching out to John was the best thing Andrew could do. Masculine Strength Males find it very hard to confide in each other. They believe that sharing their struggles makes them less of a man. But using your feminine energy to be vulnerable and trust others is the most courageous thing you can do. Masculine Strength People often feel like they are alone and have to stay strong. That's not true. When you use your feminine energy, you realize that we are all connected.

It didn't take much to get Andrew back on track. Meditating, journaling and playing the guitar helped him get in touch with his feelings and his creativity—in other words, his feminine energy. These activities helped him relax. He learned that getting ahead is not the only reason to do things–you can do things just for the pleasure of it.

Developing Your Feminine Energy

Few of us push things to the extremes as Andrew did. But if you rely too heavily on your masculine energy and you need some balance in life here are my suggestions.

Don't try to do all of them at once. Pick one or two things that you can try this week. It's better to make small but consistent baby steps than to do too much and then give up after a month.

Get in Touch with Your Emotions

Masculine Strength People suppress their emotions. They think feelings are for wimps and something they don't have time for. Like it or not, however, we are all emotional creatures. If you're not in touch with your feelings, they will manifest in unhealthy ways.

So here's an exercise to get you going. Every morning ask yourself, "How am I feeling?" Think of three words to describe it. Don't judge your feelings or analyze them; just let them be exactly what they are. It might be that you don't even know what you're feeling – this is common – but stay with it. If you give it time, your feelings will surface. Don't run away or distract yourself. Just sit with them. If this makes you feel uncomfortable, that's fine. You're a naturally courageous person so just apply your courage here. When you allow yourself to feel the discomfort, it will pass.

Express

Once you're in touch with your feelings it's time to share them. Next time you feel an emotion such as stress, anger or anxiety, call or meet up with a friend and talk about your feelings. It doesn't have to be a long conversation; simply expressing a feeling in a few sentences enables you to use your feminine energy—remember the feminine energy loves to talk. The purpose of the exercise is not to fix the problem, it is just to share.

Not only will this work wonders for your own happiness and relationships, but it can also have massive boost to your health. A study by the Harvard School of Public Health and the University of Rochester revealed that people who bottle up their emotions are 35 per cent more likely to have a premature death than those who express how they feel. Why? One theory is that when we keep a lid on how we feel, we turn to alcohol, cigarettes, junk food and drugs. Another theory is that the stress of keeping the lid on feelings affects our hormone balance, which can have a damaging effect on our health.

Ask for Help

Masculine Strength People are too proud to ask for help and don't like letting go of control. They think that asking for help is weak. They don't want to look needy or admit to others that they don't know everything. The truth is that asking for help is incredibly brave. You reveal your vulnerability, which is one of the most courageous things any of us can do. It also gives others a gift—the opportunity to show how much they care. Your relationships will blossom when you learn to use your feminine energy and lean on others.

Spend Time with Feminine Strength Friends

We pick up the energy of those around us. Spend time with Feminine Strength People. If you don't have any Feminine Strength Friends, it could be because you subconsciously judge the feminine energy as weak, superficial, silly and even sometimes stupid. This is not the truth. This is your masculine energy making you cynical and judgmental. So, make a new Feminine Strength friend. They are most likely already in your life—at work or in your extended network of friends. Take the lead;

introduce yourself and suggest meeting up for a coffee. Notice if you find yourself getting impatient with them. When this happens take a breath. Just because they go at a different pace than you do doesn't mean they are a waste of your time. My Feminine Strength Friends help me to de-stress, laugh more and remind me to take better care of myself.

Spend Time Alone

It's important to spend time alone. Masculine Strength People tend to lean toward extroversion—the masculine energy is all about how we are in the outside world. As a result, Masculine Strength People are uncomfortable being alone. However, research shows that spending time on our own makes us more creative and empathetic and it also improves our relationships with others. Schedule a bi-weekly date with yourself. Go to a cafe and read a book. Or go for a walk in the park. It will help you connect to nature, but most importantly it will help you connect to yourself. Being introspective will bring out your feminine energy.

Take a Nap

Yes, that's right—do nothing. Take a break. Put your feet up. Look out the window. Masculine Strength People think that doing nothing is indulgent, but it's in our quiet moments that some of our greatest ideas come; and by resting we perform better. Power naps of fewer than 30 minutes—even those as brief as 6 and 10 minutes—restore wakefulness and promote performance and learning. NASA found that pilots who take a 25-minute nap are 35 percent more alert and twice as focused.

Meditate

Research shows that meditation helps relieve a number of things including stress, anxiety, anger and depression. It also promotes clear and creative thinking. Sitting still and doing nothing is hell for most Masculine Strength People, but it will change everything. Try apps such as Headspace, Calm, or the Tara Brach podcast with guided meditations.

Have Massages

Not only are massages relaxing, but they have also been found to boost levels of the 'love hormone' oxytocin. Studies have revealed that oxytocin makes us more trusting and more inclined to connect with other people. It also improves empathy and monogamy – both of which are great for a highly sexed Masculine Strength Male who finds it hard to commit. Gentle massages have been found to boost oxytocin more than deep massages, so ask for soft strokes rather than an intense massage.

Get a Pet

Studies have also found that petting a dog releases oxytocin within you. It thereby helps you to bond not just with the animal but with humans too. Masculine Strength People are naturally suspicious, guarded and skeptical, but they are able to open their heart to animals, because they pose no threat. If you can't get a pet, visit animals in a shelter or farm to tap into your caring feminine energy.

Find a Creative hobby

Start a hobby that has no competitive element, like paint-ing, writing, playing an instrument, singing, photography, sculpture, or dancing. Anything that gets you spending time in your aesthetic, creative side will help you devel-op and be comfortable with your feminine energy. Such hobbies can also help you get in touch with your feelings.

Laugh

Watch comedies, or even try laughter yoga. Masculine Strength People tend to be quite serious and focused; laughter helps us to lighten up. It also helps us to bond with others. Research at the University College London has shown that that couples who laugh with each other get over tensions quicker than partners who don't. The study also found that strangers who watch a funny film together are more likely to share intimate information afterwards.

Dress Up

Experiments have shown that the clothes you wear don't just affect how other people view you. They also affect how you yourself feel and act—a phenomenon called 'en-clothed cognition.' It will be good for you to wear clothes that help you get in touch with your feminine energy. For guys, try a soft fabric sweater or a pair of up-to-date glasses. For women, try a pair of heels, a floaty, feminine skirt; or even just a piece of striking jewelry. Take care of your appearance, even when you go to bed. Treat your-self to some fancy nightwear or some sexy lingerie. Ev-ery Masculine Strength Person I know goes to bed in an old t-shirt, every Feminine Strength Person has matching pajamas.

Gentle Exercise

Most Masculine Strength People like aggressive or competitive sports. This is only going to increase your masculine energy. Instead, try gentle and fluid movement such as restorative (also called yin) yoga, tai chi, swimming and dancing. Forms of exercise like this will help you relax, breathe and be in your body. They get you connecting with yourself rather than beating someone else.

Eat Healthily

Masculine Strength People are not very aware, respectful or loving towards their bodies. They will eat pizza after a late night in the office and grab a sandwich on the go. A vital part of self-care is eating food that nourishes you. Read up on nutrition so you know the proper foods to eat and avoid. For example, when out at a restaurant choose salad or fish over steak. It will make a huge difference in how you feel. Better nutrition will also help you perform better.

Be in Nature

Being in nature will help you feel calm and still, which will help you connect to the beauty of the world. All this brings out your feminine energy. Studies have found that people who took a 90-minute walk in nature had lower levels of negative thoughts compared to those who walked in an urban setting. Such walks also boost creativity and cognitive abilities.

Unplug

Masculine Strength People don't know when to switch off. They often answer e-mails at 1:00 a.m., spend Sunday afternoons working, and never spend all of their vacation time. Make one day a week an un-plug day where you don't use any technology. Spend that day connecting with yourself, your family and friends. Go on a vacation. Your priorities in life look very different when you've had enough rest and you've enjoyed quality time with the people you love.

Acupuncture

Traditional Chinese Medicine practitioners believe that all illness comes as a result of an imbalance between yin and yang—in other words your feminine and your masculine energy. Acupuncture involves inserting very fine needles into meridian points around the body to clear blockages and facilitate the balanced flow of energy. Countless studies have shown its ability to relieve a number of things Masculine Strength People experience including anxiety, insomnia, depression, infertility, back pain, headaches and arthritis.

Heartmath

Heartmath is a fantastic training that helps you reduce stress, which can improve the quality of your life, as well as increase your lifespan. It helps you synchronize your brain and hearth for optimal stress resistance. It trains you to optimize your heartbeat to levels that are normally only possible with deep meditation and yoga. A red light flashes when your heart shows signs of stress. When this happens you know it is time to take long, deep breaths. When you are back to a healthy heart rhythm, a blue or green light appears. A green light signifies that you are in a state of high coherence. It's a great way to become aware of how stress is affecting your body and do something about it.

Have a Bath

Masculine Strength People don't like baths. Who has the time to sit around in a bubble bath all day when you can take a quick shower and get to work? Getting in touch with your feminine energy is all about slowing down and connecting with your sensual side. It is also about indulging. Treat yourself to some beautiful bath oils and rub in body lotion afterwards.

Read Fiction

At night, read a fiction book, not a business book or a biography. It will help you escape into an imaginary world for pure enjoyment. Beyond that, research from the New School for Social Research has found that reading literary fiction enhances the ability to detect and understand other people's emotions. It gives you a glimpse into people's inner worlds and helps you not to judge them, which are great ways to use your feminine energy.

Write a Journal

Studies show that expressive writing can also be a great way to get in touch with your feelings. The Five-Minute Journal is an easy way to start writing for Masculine

Strength People. Tim Ferriss is a fan. Another method is to try Morning Pages. This is when you write three pages of stream of consciousness writing first thing in the morning. Your three pages can be about anything and everything. They are to be read by no one but you. The aim is not to write anything good, but to put on paper whatever is in your head. It's a fantastic way to get in touch with your feelings and express yourself.

Listen to Music

Listening to music increases levels of oxytocin, the hormone released to help us bond with others. It also helps us to get in touch with our emotions. A study at the Free University of Berlin found that when we listen to sad songs we feel a mixture of nostalgia, peacefulness, tenderness, transcendence and wonder. Think of it as an emotional workout to pump up your feminine energy.

Be Spontaneous

Masculine Strength People love structure and can be control freaks. In order to use your feminine energy, go with the flow once in a while. If a situation arises different from what you planned, instead of fighting it and attempting to control the situation—just go with it. Be open-minded. Trust that everything will be OK. And instead of scheduling every minute of your week, leave yourself some free time—space to be spontaneous and do whatever you feel like doing that day.

"Develop the strength of a man, but live as gently as a woman."

— LAO TZU

How I Balance Myself

When I share the Bingo Theory with people, most say, "Oh, you must have so much feminine energy because you like fashion and beauty. You are always dressed up and have make-up on. You're so easy-going, fun and kind." They're right. I do have those qualities. But they don't always come naturally. I'm a actually a Masculine Strength Female.

As a kid growing up in Azerbaijan I was a tomboy. I had no interest in hair or make-up. I loved wearing jeans, playing with boys, climbing trees and running around. Leyla, my sister, was the girlie one who always wore dresses and sat around talking with her girl friends.

Only in my teenage years did I develop any interest in beauty or fashion. I remember the day I wore my first skirt. It was a check kilt that my grandpa bought me— and I loved it. As soon as I put it on, I felt different. I realized that when I took care of my appearance I felt better and the world responded differently to me. I was expressing my feminine energy for the first time.

When I was sixteen, we moved to Toronto, Canada.

Moving to the other side of the world, where my parents had no jobs, and none of us had any family or friends was very challenging.

There was one moment that I'll never forget. I had just started to make friends at school and I asked my parents for money to go to the movies one weekend. They said they were sorry but they didn't have the money. It must have been so difficult for them to say that to their daughter, but in that moment I only saw my own pain.

I locked myself up in my room and cried for the rest of the evening. I blamed my parents. I felt sorry for myself, and I worried about what my new friends would think of me.

That evening something very formative happened. After crying for hours into a pillow, I calmed down and wiped the tears from my red, puffy face. I took a deep breath and sighed. I realized in that moment that if I wanted anything in life, I'd have to get it myself. I couldn't rely on anyone but myself.

When I had that recognition I felt this immense strength inside of me —it was my masculine energy.

Shortly after that I found a bit of work babysitting and then got a job at a fast-food chain. The new jobs were tough at first, but I was grateful to make my own money and to feel independent. It felt empowering.

For the next six years I split my time between several jobs and school. I worked in a bank in the morning, went to school in the afternoon, and waitressed at night. I had no days off, no weekends.

With the money I brought in I helped my parents pay mortgage on our new house. I was so proud of myself.

But the cracks started to show. Whenever I had a few hours off I felt lost and overwhelmed. I didn't know what to do when I wasn't working.

And then I burned out. I had a mid life crisis at the age of 22! Or a quarter life crisis, I guess. I was exhausted, empty and anxious. I would look in the mirror in the washroom at work and ask myself, "What's the point of all of this? Why am I even here?"

I had pains in my chest and heart palpitations. I couldn't go on like this any longer. I needed some time for reflection. I no longer saw the purpose of anything.

My first burnout was a wake-up call. It was my feminine energy demanding that I slow down and look after myself.

I started to care more about what I ate and drank, and I began to exercise regularly. I realized that I had to find work that would help me become balanced so I trained to be an image consultant. I loved the creative challenges of fashion and I loved helping people. But I was also decisive and clear in my advice—and I had no problem charging people for my time. Without realizing it, I used both my masculine and feminine energies. That's why I enjoyed it so much.

Years later, I still live my life in a way that allows me to use both my masculine and feminine energies.

Not only at work but also in my personal life.

In the business I now have with my husband, I mainly manage the creative part of things because it makes me happy and further develops my feminine energy. I could do the books – that comes easily to me but I know it will make me miserable. Instead, I focus my energy on the creative work and styling for our products, videos and photography. Of course there is so much more that I do on a daily basis, although I have to admit— that's my favorite part.

As a Masculine Strength Female, I find it hard to express my emotions and feelings. My YouTube videos push me to face my fears and talk openly about my thoughts, feelings, dreams and ideas.

But it takes constant effort. My natural strength is always going to be my masculine energy. It's easy for me to make business decisions, have a clear vision, manage people and lead people to do what needs to be done. My natural style is to push myself, to work harder.

It takes constant effort for me to learn how to sugar coat things and be gentler when I communicate with staff. My tendency is to be blunt and aggressive because the masculine energy is always direct. It's my natural tendency to tell someone, "This isn't good enough!" Instead I make a conscious effort to start my conversations by saying, "So I noticed this needs to be changed…"

In my personal life, I learned that I love feeding people. It makes me feel nurturing. It's my way of showing that I care. I also hug people more. I used to be reserved. But it feels good to hug because it taps into my feminine energy. It brings out the connectedness, the compassion and the love in me.

I now go for regular massages, acupunctures and sometimes even facials—something that would never have been a priority before. I meditate for a minimum of 10 minutes every morning and evening. It has profound effect on my day. It helps me feel calm, relaxed and peaceful.

Spending time with animals also helps me tremendously. If I see a cat or dog on the street, I'll sit down to pet it, because I can feel how it opens my heart—and that's the joy of life.

I don't want to only have masculine energy and I don't want to only have feminine energy – I want to experience both. We are all capable of doing that.

I want to go from super-powerful, get-things-done mode, to being there when a friend needs me mode. I want to be kind and compassionate but firm in my communications. Like a good handshake, that is neither too gentle, nor too strong. The balance makes all the difference. The art is in knowing when to use my masculine energy and when to use my feminine energy. It's a dance. And it's beautiful.

SUMMARY

BECOMING A BINGO FOR MASCULINE STRENGTH MEN AND WOMEN

IN THE LAST SECTION you learned how to become more balanced. But this will only work only if you take action—slow, steady, consistent action.

It's important to understand that this is not a quick fix. We must continue to maintain this balance throughout our lives.

We are always changing. We are all made of energy and energy is always flowing through us. There will be times when you use more masculine energy and times when you use more feminine.

As you become more balanced, you will learn to dance between the two energies and use whichever one is appropriate for the situation.

If you are a Feminine Strength Person, your task is to bring out your masculine energy by being more assertive, focused and organized. Make a plan. Get up and do something. Do anything.

When you combine these skills with your own natural

fun, love and creativity, you will feel energy and confidence that you never had before. You will use your head as well as your heart. You will be strong yet gentle. This is a winning combination, a Bingo!

If you are a Masculine Strength Person, your challenge is to bring out your feminine energy by being less controlling and more open. You must learn to get in touch with your feelings and connect with others. You must learn to stop *doing* and learn to just *be*.

When you use your heart as well as your head, your life will open up to you. It will be like going from black and white to a rainbow of colors. You will have passion, love and peace in your life. You will be that winning combination, a Bingo!

When you have both energies you become a Bingo. Then you're ready to meet the partner of your dreams and have your Bingo relationship—a relationship that's entirely different from the kind of relationships most people have in the world today.

IV

PART FOUR

The Bingo Relationship

.....

"Your task is not to seek for love, but merely to seek and find all the barriers within yourself that you have built against it."

— RUMI

11

OPPOSITES ATTRACT

MOST RELATIONSHIPS are based on fear—fear of losing the other person, fear that you're not good enough, fear that *they* are not good enough. This fear makes us crazy. This fear makes us feel powerless and desperate. It makes us do things we shouldn't do and accept behavior we shouldn't accept.

Why the fear?

Well, for years we've looked to others to complete us. Masculine Strength People have looked to Feminine Strength People to provide them with love, nurturing and wisdom.

Feminine Strength People have looked to Masculine Strength People to protect them, and take control.

In some ways this might sound like it makes sense – after all, it's why people often refer to their partners as their "other half." And it might even work—for some time.

You meet someone and there's chemistry. "This is it!" you think. I feel complete! He or she meets all my needs!

Then, before too long, fear starts to creep in. You start to worry that this person may leave you— the person who fulfills all your needs—may leave you. You panic. You become jealous and controlling. You behave in ways you hope will make them stay. You tolerate bad behavior because you're afraid of being on your own again.

Then as time goes by something else happens. You start to feel dissatisfied. You realize that even though you're clinging to this relationship, you still don't feel complete. They're not doing enough. They're not behaving the right way. They're not good enough. You get angry and frustrated with them. You nag and manipulate them. You try to control them.

The relationship continues with an under current of bitterness and resentment – or it ends and you look for someone new. You then repeat the pattern. You always look to other people to make you feel whole and wonder why it never works out.

This kind of relationship – the kind that many of us are in – is not love. It's an arrangement with a contract that says, "If you behave this way, then I'll love you and if I behave that way, then you'll love me." But this never works out. Why? Because nobody can make us feel whole – or make us feel love - except ourselves.

When you balance yourself—when you become a Bingo—you attract a different kind of relationship. When you're a Bingo you don't need anyone to complete you. You're already complete. You don't need anyone to make you happy. You're already happy. And you don't need anyone to love you. You already love yourself and everyone around you.

Instead, you love for the sake of loving. You love unconditionally, expecting nothing in return.

The Magical Kitchen

There's a beautiful story that explains unconditional love in one of my favorite books, *The Mastery of Love* by Don Miguel Ruiz.

It asks you to imagine that you have a magical kitchen in your house that provides you with all the food you need, all the time.

Because you have so much, you are happy to share it with others – not because you want anything in return, but just because it feels good to share.

Then one day somebody knocks on the door with a pizza. They offer to give you a slice, as long as you are nice to them and do exactly what they say.

How do you react? You already have all the food you need—including pizza—so you tell them you don't need their food, but they're welcome to come in and eat whatever they like. And they don't need to do anything for the food, because you just like to share.

Now imagine a different situation. Here you have no magical kitchen. In fact weeks have gone by and you have not eaten. You're starving. The same person comes offering pizza under the same terms. When you smell it, your tummy rumbles.

You agree to do anything for just one slice. You eat it and it tastes good. You're offered more tomorrow so long as you keep doing what they ask you to do. Again, you agree to anything. You get so used to having the food that you start to worry it will be taken away. What if my partner gives it to someone else?

In this story, the food represents love.

Your heart is like the magical kitchen. When it is full of love, you don't need anyone else's love. There's no need to go begging for love. You already have all the love you need. You share your love without condition because you have so much of it.

On the other hand, what happens if you're starving for love? Then you'll agree to anything. You'll desperately cling to the person who offers you love, and you'll be terrified of losing it. You'll even accept all kinds of bad behavior—and do some bad behaving of your own—just to keep the love.

Giving Rather Than Taking

When you are a Bingo, you won't sign up for the kind of love that will not make you happy. Why would you?

You've learned how to develop and express both energies within yourself, and you don't need someone else to make you feel whole. You're already whole.

If you're a Feminine Strength Bingo, you don't need to find a Masculine Strength Person to provide for you financially, or protect you, or make your plans. You can do that yourself by using the masculine energy that exists inside of you.

And if you're a Masculine Strength Bingo, you don't need someone else to love and care for you because you know how to love and care for yourself. You simply draw on the feminine energy that dwells inside of you.

There are no holes to fill. You're complete. You have

the Magic Kitchen and will never be hungry.

When you're a Bingo you won't enter relationships out of fear and neediness; you go into them to give rather than to take. You have all the love you could ever need inside of you. And you have all the power and strength as well. Now you want to share that energy with the world—with no conditions.

Interdependence Versus Co-dependence

So does that mean that you don't need anybody? That you don't need a relationship?

No, far from it. Human beings are here to love each other and to connect. We are interdependent social creatures.

And interdependence is very different from dependence.

When we are interdependent, we are whole and balanced within ourselves. We are able to live on our own and provide for ourselves, but we *choose* to share our life and love with others because it makes us feel happy and helps us grow.

When we are dependent or co-dependent we go into relationships because we need other people to provide us with something we don't have.

But as we've learned, we have everything within us—we just need to find it. This is why it's so important that we improve on our relationship with ourselves before we concern ourselves with a relationship with someone else.

It is only when you realize that you are complete in yourself that you can *really* love unconditionally; wanting nothing in return. Then your love comes from abundance not fear. You love because you want to share.

INTERDEPENDENCE DYNAMIC

DEPENDENCE DYNAMIC

DEPENDENCE - INTERDEPENDENCE DIAGRAM

In the diagram, you see illustrated three entities - Identity of Person A (Him), Identity of Person B (Her) and the resulting relationship.

The essence of the idea here is that both people come into a relationship feeling whole, complete and filled with self-love. They don't need each other, they just love each other. They are able to nurture and sustain themselves; the dynamic between them is one of deep respect, admiration and care. This is the **Interdependent Dynamic** which can feel like magic. This is what is often meant when people say their relationship feels natural and effortless.

The flip side of the Interdependent dynamic is the **Dependent Dynamic**. The underlying assumption there is that both people need each other to be complete. For example - Rachel might think Josh doesn't love her because he doesn't come jogging with her because that's really important to her. She feels that he is responsible for making her feel loved. Making the other person responsible for how you feel is the core of what is behind the dependent dynamic. This leads to unhealthy behavior such as blame and escalating arguments, due to lack of both people taking responsibility for their feelings.

As you see, a significant difference between both diagrams is that the identity of Person A (him) and Person B (her) are clearly defined in Interdependence while they are more loosely defined in Dependence. A core function of independence is taking re-sponsibility for one's thoughts and emotions and subsequent self regulation (being able to calm oneself down in an argument, being able to de-stress without letting it spill onto the other person,etc. This makes the relationship simpler, more loving and ultimately wonderful for both sides.

When you get to that wonderful place, who will you want to share your love with?

Opposites Attract

You know how they say opposites attract? That's very true. However, it's not opposite *personalities* that attract. If one person loves travelling the world but the other is a home bird, that will eventually put a strain on the relationship. You won't have enough in common to make it last long term.

When we say opposites attract, what we mean is opposite *energies.*

Have you ever felt that chemistry with someone? That incredible, electric feeling? That's what happens when the masculine and feminine energies connect with each other.

In science, the attraction of opposites is called polarity; it's what's behind magnetism.

In the same way that opposite poles of a magnet are attracted to each other, in romantic relationships opposite energies are attracted to each other.

It doesn't matter whether the feminine energy is the strength of the man or the woman in the relationship. Just as it doesn't matter whether the masculine energy is the strength of the woman or the man in the relationship. There just needs to be a polarity. Both energies need to be present. That's when there's passion, excitement, energy—and great sex.

The feminine energy flirts, plays and seduces. The masculine energy brings strength, power and action. The feminine energy receives; the masculine energy gives.

The masculine energy takes control, and the feminine energy follows, lovingly.

This is about more than just physical attraction.

We're all attracted to our opposite energies because it helps us see what we're missing. Relationships act like mirrors. They reflect back what we need to learn. You know the phrase monkey see, monkey do? That's how we are in relationships. We see something and we start to mimic it.

If you're a Masculine Strength Person and you spend a lot of time with the feminine energy, it will rub off on you. You'll observe your partner's love, openness and spontaneity and learn from it.

Likewise, if you're a Feminine Strength Person you will see your Masculine Strength partner's drive, energy and focus, and you will want to be more like that.

When we spend time with someone who's the opposite energy to us, it helps to bring out that energy in us. On the other hand, if we see more of what we already are it doesn't help us. We amplify our dominant energy instead of balancing it.

In many cases we're drawn to people who have the same strength energy. This is natural because, after all, we have so much in common. But these relationships rarely help us to grow.

Whether it's with your partner or with your friends or family, the purpose of relationships is to help us evolve as humans. The relationships that help us grow the most are the ones with our opposites. Together you learn from each other and grow.

Take a moment to look at your relationships with your

friends. In most cases your best friend is an opposite energy to you. As a Masculine Strength Female, most of my friends are Feminine Strength Females. It's not something I consciously set out to do—it's just something that's happened because I like the way I feel around the feminine energy.

These friends challenge me and teach me a lot about life, self-love and acceptance. They're fun to be around, and they teach me how to take it easy, take care of myself, and enjoy the finer things in life. They teach me how to have fun and just BE—rather than always DO.

And it works both ways. My friends tell me that I make them feel more confident and clear about what they need to do. They feel energized by being with me. We learn from each other.

If you look at your friendships and see that they are all the same strength energy as you, then it's time to broaden your circle and make new friends.

We Still Need to Balance

Even though opposites attract and help each other balance out we must always continue to work on balancing ourselves while we're in the relationship. If we don't learn to embrace the weaker energy within us, we will find it very hard accept that energy in our partner.

For example, if you're a Feminine Strength Female and you haven't learned to use your masculine energy you might be scared by the energy of the Masculine Strength Male. You might worry that it's overpowering, aggressive or cold. It's only by getting in touch with your own masculine power—by learning how to be assertive and strong—that you can accept it in others.

Likewise, if you're a Masculine Strength Female and you haven't learned to accept your emotional, creative, softer feminine energy, you may act like a bully to your partner when he expresses his feminine energy.

Being balanced does not mean that you become androgynous

You might worry that if you both balance your energies you will lose the polarity, but it doesn't work like that.

Your natural strength will always be your natural strength, no matter how well you develop your opposite energy. I'm pretty well balanced after years of working on myself, but my masculine energy is still my strength and it always will be. My husband, Alex's natural strength, on the other hand, will always be his feminine energy— which is why our relationship works so well.

Does this mean I can't love someone with the same energy?

It's easy to love someone with the same energy as you but attraction is a different matter. Opposites always have and always will attract in a way that the same energy will not. So does that mean that if you are already in a relationship with the same energy that it's doomed to fail? Not at all. I'll show you how such relationships can evolve into a beautiful and balanced companionship in the following chapters.

Are you ready to find your Bingo relationship?

In the next chapters I will tell you how to start looking for a balanced relationship if you're single. It's Bingo dating! If you're in a partnership, you can skip ahead to the Bingo Relationship chapters where you'll learn how to balance your existing relationships.

PART FIVE

Bingo
Dating

.....

A COUPLE OF YEARS AGO I was out shopping with my friend, Selina. It was a beautiful spring afternoon and we were sitting in a cafe talking about the guy that Selina had just started dating.

"He's perfect," she said. "He's sweet, fun, spontaneous. We can talk for hours, but... I don't know why, I just don't feel any chemistry."

"Is he good-looking?" I asked.

"Yes, he's really good-looking! And so well dressed. He keeps getting me little gifts and he's really into me ... but it just doesn't feel right."

She took a sip of her mango smoothie and said, "Maybe it's because he's short ..."

"You've gone out with other guys who are short and there was chemistry," I said.

"So why do you think it isn't working?" she asked me. "I'm 30. I want a relationship, and on paper this guy is everything I'd like but I just don't feel it."

I've had this conversation with countless single friends

before. Both men and women talk about this moment when they meet a person who's perfect—and yet they don't feel it.

And I tell them why it's not working. They're going out with people who have the same energy. There is no polarity, no attraction.

Selina found a guy who was sweet, fun and spontaneous. Someone who could talk for hours and always looked great—all wonderful qualities. There was only one problem. They were the same qualities that she had.

What Selina needed was a Masculine Strength Male. I know other girls who are driven and successful Masculine Strength Females and they're always looking for people who are as driven as they are – in other words they're looking for a Masculine Strength Male. But when they find them it often doesn't work out.

The following chapters are for those of you who may have had conversations similar to the one Selina had with me, those of you who are single and looking.

In this section I'll show you how the Masculine and Feminine Strength singles that we've followed throughout the book changed their approach in dating.

They've already worked hard to balance themselves.

Their lives changed in ways they did not expect. They feel different, they feel more fulfilled, and the world responds to them differently. In fact, it feels like the world opened up for them—in both their personal and professional lives.

Now it's time to find and give love. But how?

"Male and female represent the two sides of the great radical dualism. But in fact they are perpetually passing into one another. Fluid hardens to solid, solid rushes to fluid. There is no wholly masculine man, no purely feminine woman."

— MARGARET FULLER

12

DATING TIPS FOR THE FEMININE STRENGTH FEMALE

BEFORE Lily took on her new job and started to develop her masculine energy, her love life was a mess. She met guys easily, because her curvy figure and open, feminine energy drew men to her. But her relationships never went anywhere... except the bedroom. Let's see how that changed when she started to become more balanced within herself.

All Lily wanted to do was fall in love, settle down and start a family – ideally with a wealthy, successful guy. For years, though she'd ended up with the bad boys who had no interest in anything more than casual sex.

It wasn't that she didn't like the sex – she did. And she liked the excitement too. The guys she met were never boring; they had a lot of ambition and big ideas. They always seemed to be doing something – except, that is, committing to her.

Her last boyfriend even cheated on her and she put up with it thinking he'd change his ways with time. He didn't.

There was one guy who drove her crazy. He was a hot shot in the tech industry. They met at a party and hit it off. They had great sex that night—and great conversation too. Lily hoped it would become something but he was always travelling for work. Whenever they saw each other it seemed to end up in bed. He always paid for dinner and was generous—that made her feel good but it also made her feel a bit cheap.

When he was away, Lily went on dates with nice guys – guys who wanted to see the same exhibitions and movies that interested her. They were sweet and attentive but there was never any real spark. Sometimes she wondered if she should settle for one of them—at least they wouldn't hurt her.

Lily was a nice, smart, attractive woman – what was she doing wrong?

Getting her new job, however, changed everything. For the first few months she was too busy to even think about men. Work took all of her attention.

By the time she started dating again she felt different. She was getting a grip on her own finances and so for the first time she wasn't looking for a Prince Charming to rescue her.

She also felt stronger and more confident in herself. She realized that she didn't need to jump into bed with a guy to make him like her. In fact, she was done with doing that.

One night her tech hotshot called to let her know he was in town. It was a booty call. She told him she had other plans and that their "thing"—whatever it was—wasn't working for her. She wanted a serious relationship and if that wasn't what he wanted then it was time for them both to move on.

She heard his stunned silence on the other end of the phone. He told her that he really liked her and wanted something more serious but he just couldn't at the moment with work being so crazy. She knew he could never give her what she wanted or needed so she said good-bye.

When she hung up the phone Lily felt a rush of energy. She had never felt so empowered. She had stood up for herself, something she had never done before.

From that moment on, Lily radiated an aura of confidence she didn't have before. She didn't end up in one-night stands because she was no longer attracted to those kinds of guys. She wanted more, and she knew, for the first time in her life, that she deserved more.

Shortly afterwards, she met Mike at a fitness boot camp. He was an engineer who was not interested in any of the things she was interested in – but he was interested in her. He didn't try to get her into bed with fancy dinners and big promises; he just kept showing up.

Every time they arranged to go out, he turned up on time and did what he said he would. On paper they had nothing in common but it just worked. He listened to her. His eyes lit up whenever she walked into the room. She felt safe with him. He was reliable and loyal and straight-forward.

But Lily felt scared as well. He was strong and real—there was no pretending. She had never met anyone like him before. They didn't have sex until their fifth date – but when they did it just felt right. This is it, thought Lily. He is the one.

When you're not balanced, you will attract people who are just as unbalanced as you. When Lily only used her feminine energy, she met guys who only used their masculine energy - in other words, Masculine Strength Males who were only interested in sex.

Feminine Strength Females love sex too, and because they are naturally open it's easy for them to fall into bed. But this rarely leads to anything more than hook-ups. And as much as the Feminine Strength Female likes to pretend she's OK with that, she's not. Her priorities are love, trust and connection, after all.

The Feminine Strength Female might tolerate a lot of bad behavior because she has a forgiving nature and hates confrontation, but in the end she gets hurt. This is when she does one of two things: she puts on a protective, masculine shell and pretends that she doesn't care, or she turns to a nice Feminine Strength Guy who might seem safe but who will never really excite her. There isn't enough polarity there for real attraction.

When Lily started to use her masculine energy in the office – and also at the gym – things changed. She felt more powerful and more confident.

Her first major step was to end it with her on-off guy. She took control and stood up for herself with the help of her masculine energy.

Once she started respecting herself, other people respected her more. Remember, our relationships with others always reflect our relationship with ourselves.

Notice that a big boost to Lily's confidence happened when she took control of her money situation. Feminine Strength Females find it hard to manage their finances. They often wait to find a partner to do that for them. When Lily started to manage her own money she realized she didn't need to put up with bad behavior in exchange for a few fancy dinners. It's fine to let a guy pay—and many Masculine Strength Males want to provide—but you must never give away your power or become dependent on another person.

Then Lily met Mike, a balanced Masculine Strength Male. On paper Lily and Mike have different lives. She is artsy, creative and feminine; he's practical, down-to-earth and straight talking. At first, he didn't seem as exciting as the other guys she'd dated, but over time she saw that he offered much more than they did. He adored her, but he also respected her—something that was lacking in previous relationships. And for the first time in her life she respected herself enough to know that she deserved a guy as good as Mike.

Can You Relate?

Have you found yourself endlessly giving to guys that don't commit? Do you put up with bad behavior in a relationships just because you want love?

Or maybe you're a Feminine Strength Female who thinks, "I'd never let a man mess me around! And I don't want any guy to pay for me! I have my own money."

We live in a world where we are told that men and women should be equal partners, and that's absolutely right. But equality can also be damaging to relationships if it means that you, as a Feminine Strength Female, are acting in ways that are not true to your nature.

Many Feminine Strength Women rely on their masculine energy when they're dating (and indeed when they're working) as a way of not getting hurt. They play hard-to-get, and don't let men see their vulnerable side. They give men career advice on dates and jump into bed. But this is not their true nature. And they will never attract the right guy behaving like this.

It might also be that you've had bad experiences or traumas with Masculine Strength Men—including, perhaps, your father. So you decide to use your masculine energy to protect yourself. You might go out with sweet, nice Feminine Strength Males because they feel safer to you – but these relationships will never give you what you need.

So what do you need?

Your Bingo Partner

Forget macho guys who use you or sweet Feminine Strength Males who bore you. You need a strong, loyal, reliable, balanced Masculine Strength Male. Don't be put off by the fact that this guy might be quiet and understated. That's what real confidence looks like, not the flashy showiness of the unbalanced masculine energy on an ego trip.

How To Find It

GET OUT THERE

Prince Charming is not going to come to your house and sweep you off your feet, so get off the sofa and get out there—and that doesn't mean go shopping with girlfriends or hang out in fancy cocktail bars. Go places where Masculine Strength Males hang out, like sporting events, the gym, or business networking events.

FLIRT

As a Feminine Strength Female attracting people comes naturally. So use your strength! Be open, flirtatious, fun and easy going. The secret to flirting is eye contact and smiling. If you see a guy you like, smile and hold his gaze for a second more than is comfortable. Then look away and look back at him, with a playful smile. This makes it clear that if he approaches you he won't be rejected.

DO NOT MAKE THE FIRST MOVE

This tip is really important. Yes, we live in an equal world and there's no reason why women can't make the first move, but if you are a Feminine Strength Female looking for a Masculine Strength Male, you have to do it the old-fashioned way. Remember, the masculine energy wants to take charge; the feminine energy wants to receive. Your job is to make it easy for the guy to approach you, to lure him in. If that means sitting near him, or walking past him – that's fine. But make sure he talks first. If you make the first move and he likes it, chances are he's not a Masculine Strength Man.

DON'T BE AFRAID TO GO OUT WITH SOMEONE DIFFERENT FROM YOU

If you meet a guy you can talk with for hours, someone

who loves the same art as you and has read the same books, he's probably a Feminine Strength Male. That makes for a wonderful connection and a wonderful friendship – but not sexual chemistry. Remember you're looking for your opposite. Don't be put off by the fact that you might not, at first, have a lot in common. You'll find other ways to connect, and you'll learn and grow from each other. He might not be book smart but he'll be street-smart. And he might not recognize beauty in art – but he'll recognize it in you and that's what matters.

KNOW WHEN TO LISTEN AND WHEN TO TALK

We all know the Feminine Strength Female can talk for hours – but make sure you give your date a chance to talk too. Masculine Strength Males can be more re-served, so make an effort to draw them out. Ask them questions and show real interest. If, on the other hand, your date is talking over you— it's probably an attempt to impress you. Don't be afraid to speak up. You might think that it's your job to be "nice" but guys like a wom-an who stands up for herself. Don't be a push over.

LET HIM PAY

The masculine energy's role is to give, and the feminine energy's role is to receive – so let the guy pay for dinner, at least initially. This doesn't mean you're signing up to be a 1950s housewife. Nor does it mean you're not capa-ble of paying for yourself. Further down the line you can split bills, but when you are first dating, let the guy pay. And no, it does not mean you have to jump into bed with him. Just because a guy pays for dinner does not mean you owe him anything.

SLOW DOWN

It's so exciting when you meet someone you like. A great first date is enough to have you picking out names for your first-born. The feminine energy is open and spontaneous – it falls in love easily. But this time, take it slow. Don't give your heart away too quickly. The feminine energy is so open that you can get hurt when you give away your heart too quickly and to the wrong person.

DON'T JUMP INTO BED

Sex is important in any relationship, but it can wait. The best relationships are built on friendship. What's the rush? Get to know him first and let him get to know you. Build anticipation and desire. If you wait, sex will be even better because it will be more meaningful. It will also send an important message to him. You don't just do it with anyone. He's special and so are you. This is how you exercise your masculine energy. Instead of allowing yourself to be dictated by your emotions and what feels right in the moment, use your logic and discipline.

DON'T RELY ON INTERNET DATING

Make sure you're not only dating online. There are definitely great guys online but you'll find a lot of Feminine Strength Males who lack the confidence to approach women in real life. And there are also a lot of unbalanced Masculine Strength Males looking for a hook-up.

Neither guy is right for you. You'll end up with endless messages that never go anywhere (with the Feminine Strength Male) or you might end up in bed with a guy who isn't looking for anything serious.

USE YOUR INTUITION

Always trust your intuition—it's your strength after all. If the relationship isn't working out, be honest with yourself and leave it as soon as possible. It's not your job to fix or mold this person into what you want him to be. You can't change anyone—neither do you have the right to change someone. Let him live his life the way he wants to. You will find someone who is right for you.

TRUST

Trust should come naturally to Feminine Strength Females but if you've been hurt by a Masculine Strength Male before it's so easy to put up a barrier. Please don't do this. Remember that by using your intuition and working on your masculine energy, you gain the strength to look after yourself in relationships. It's only by surrendering and trusting that you will find true love.

KEEP USING YOUR MASCULINE ENERGY

Even when you're in a happy, healthy relationship, continue to nurture and balance both your masculine and feminine energies. Remember that nobody else can make you whole; you need to do that yourself. When you first meet the right guy, it will be tempting to give up working on yourself. You'll think that he's the answer to all your problems. He's not. It's important that you keep working on yourself in order to have a happy relationship and a happy life.

13

DATING TIPS FOR THE
FEMININE STRENGTH MALE

AND NOW let's catch up with Chris, our Feminine Strength Male. Chris has no problem talking to women but he has a problem asking them out. He's spent most of his life in the friend-zone – so how did he get out of it? Like Lily, things changed for him when he started to use his masculine energy.

Chris's business with Harry really started to get somewhere. He felt a sense of control over his life that he'd never felt before. He felt inspired but grounded at the same time. It was a cool feeling. Now he wanted to share that feeling with someone else.

There was a girl he liked in his office building but he hadn't found the courage to ask her out. Her name was Amy and she was an accountant. She was an athletic brunette – exactly his type, physically. Her personality was great too – she was direct and strong. She said it how she saw it. He loved that in a woman. He couldn't get on with girlie girls.

He thought she liked him too. He sent her funny little e-mails and they seemed to make her laugh. But he didn't know if she liked him romantically or just as a friend – and he was too scared to make a move.

He played it out in his head, again and again, thinking about how he might ask her and where he might do it. But he kept coming back to the same thing: what would happen if she said 'no'?

Most of his single guy friends had no problem approaching girls but he hated it. Once they broke the ice, Chris was always good at joining in and keeping the conversation going, but he could never make the first move.

His last two relationships both started when the girls asked him out. He had no problem with that—in fact, he thought it was cool.

His last relationship lasted four years. He loved that she was strong and confident but soon he started feeling like he was being bossed around. It felt emasculating. There was no tenderness or romance from her side.

It took him a long time to get the courage to finally break it off— he hated hurting anyone. Still, he knew it was the right thing to do.

Since then he ended up in the friend's zone with most of the girls he met. He'd meet a girl he liked and he'd hang out with her. But he'd never make a move and, so she'd just think they were friends.

He was getting frustrated. He needed to man up and ask Amy out. Then one day he saw his opportunity. They were talking about an art exhibition that was soon closing.

"We should go," she said, casually. He didn't know if she meant as friends or as a date but it didn't matter. He said he'd get the tickets. He texted her when he'd got them and said, "See you outside the gallery, Saturday at 1pm." He felt bold. He was taking control.

They went to the exhibition. He saw a silly keychain in the gift shop, so he bought it for her. He didn't know if that was too cheesy of a move or not. He kept thinking of his guy friends telling him to play it cool—but he still gave it to her and she loved it.

They went for a coffee afterwards and then walked in the park. He still didn't know if it was a date or if they were just friends but he knew he had to do something to find out. They were sitting down on a bench, feeding the ducks when he leaned in to kiss her. She kissed him right back.

The Feminine Strength Male is open and sweet and tender but he is not good at making the first move. It doesn't matter how much confidence he has in other areas of life; this is something that he finds challenging. He fears embarrassment and rejection and over-thinks all the things that could go wrong.

That's why online dating works for him – the stakes are lower. Nobody is watching if he gets rejected. Also, it's easier for his personality to shine through on witty messages rather than face-to-face. That's why it worked for Chris to send Amy funny e-mails. He could build a relationship slowly.

The problem with the Feminine Strength Male, though, is that they move so slowly, the girl assumes they are just friends.

Before Chris learned to use his masculine energy he met girls who were as unbalanced as he was. His ex-girlfriend had very strong masculine energy – which was great because she made the first move - but then it stopped working because she became too aggressive and cold (going too much into the masculine energy) and he became increasingly passive and timid (going too much into the feminine).

Chris needed to step into his masculine energy in order to find a balanced relationship. Everything changed for him when he used his masculine energy to make his business a success. He felt a confidence and sense of control he hadn't felt before—enough confidence, at least, to act on Amy's passing comment that she'd like to see the exhibition.

Amy, as a Masculine Strength Female, was forward enough to give him the green light by suggesting they go to the exhibition – but he still had to have the courage to take it from there, which he did. Getting the tickets was a confident, masculine move—as was moving in for a kiss. But Chris also drew on his romantic feminine energy when he bought her a gift. He knew that his Masculine Strength Friends would never do that but he followed his heart and did it. She loved him for it.

Can You Relate?

Do you find yourself in the friend's zone? Do you find yourself paralyzed when it comes to making the first move? Do you wish you could be like your other guy friends, who seem to talk to any girl they want without worrying? Do you love powerful women but sometimes get bullied by them?

Until you learn to step into your masculine energy, you're going to attract unbalanced Masculine Strength Females. As soon as you work on your own confidence and take control, you will find the right match for you, who is as balanced as you are.

Your Bingo Partner

You need a strong and confident Masculine Strength Female who is kind and balanced. Somebody who knows what she wants and isn't afraid to ask for it. She is the kind of woman who makes things happen and makes you feel energized – but not emasculated - when you're with her.

How To Get It

DON'T PLAY GAMES

If you want to find love and get into a healthy relationship you need to accept yourself and own your feminine energy. Too many men have been brainwashed into acting macho and playing games when it comes to dating. This is not authentic to you. Rule Number One is drop all games and be yourself. The right woman for you will love you just the way you are.

The notion that 'nice guys finish last' was invented by Masculine Strength Men. You're nice, kind and romantic and that is your strength in a relationship. The right woman will love and appreciate these qualities in you.

DO NOT BULK UP

You don't need to bulk up in order to meet the right woman for you. So many Feminine Strength Males think they need to go to the gym, use heavy weights and drink protein shakes in order to look like a muscleman in order to attract the ladies. Most Masculine Strength Females aren't into bulky men. We love lean – but fit, nerdy men. Glasses are a bonus!

ASK HER OUT

Your dream woman is someone who takes charge and makes the first move but so many women, even Masculine Strength Females, have been conditioned to think that guys have to do the asking. Step your game up and be more proactive. If you like someone, ask her out. Waiting too long might turn a woman off, because she thinks you aren't really interested in her. If a woman makes a hint about wanting to see a film or go to an exhibit that's your queue – take charge and make plans. Set a date.

GO ONLINE

Online dating works for you. It allows you to chat with girls without having to go up to them in a bar - something you hate. Messages are a good way to show your sweet, funny side. Also, women may feel more comfortable making the first move online.

KISS HER

Don't be afraid to kiss her on the first date to show her that you are interested. Because you get on with women naturally it's not always obvious whether you're sexually attracted to a girl or you're just hanging out as friends. If you don't make a move she'll think you're not interested, and you'll end up in the friend zone.

TELL HER HOW YOU FEEL

As the relationship progresses, be honest and open about your feelings. This is where you can exercise both your masculine and feminine energies; expressing love is feminine but having the guts to do so verbally and directly is masculine. Don't be afraid to be the first to say "I love you" if that's how you feel—if you're dating a Masculine Strength Female she most likely won't be the first to openly express her feelings for you.

KEEP USING YOUR MASCULINE ENERGY

Even when you're in a happy, healthy relationship, continue to nurture and balance both your masculine and feminine energies. Remember that nobody else can make you whole. You need to do that yourself. When you first meet the right girl, it will be tempting to give up working on yourself. You'll think that she's the answer to all your problems. She's not. It's important that you keep working on yourself in order to have a happy relationship and a happy life.

14

DATING TIPS FOR THE MASCULINE STRENGTH FEMALE

REMEMBER CHLOE, the lawyer who was passed up for a promotion and used it as an opportunity to get work-life balance? Well, her life changed in every single way the day she decided to take some time off work. It started with her love life.

While Chloe worked the crazy hours on her mission to become a partner, she also tried to date. Not surprisingly it did not go well. She terrified most men she met, telling more than a couple of them to "just get to the point" with their stories.

One guy joked that he felt like he was on a job interview. Another one accused her of being a "ball-breaker."

She thought men were intimidated by her success and intelligence but she was damned if she was going to play down her achievements.

She looked for her Alpha male match – someone with his own place, a good job, and a good body - but these guys didn't seem interested in her. The way she saw it, they just wanted a bimbo.

She went out with a couple of sweet guys she met on-line, although she was more successful than they were career-wise. She liked talking to them but they didn't have the guts to make the moves, and that annoyed her. Did she have to do everything?

She went out with one guy three times and he was sweet but he still didn't have the courage to kiss her. In the end she got fed up of waiting. She texted him to say it wasn't working. He texted back to say that he was really disappointed, but what did he expect? He missed his chance.

When she got passed up for the partnership at the firm, Chloe reassessed everything.

She took a three-month long sabbatical and went to Asia.

For twelve perfect weeks she lived in a sarong, laid in hammocks and hung out with the kind of people she would not have met in her normal life. She had a lot of time to think – which wasn't always fun. She could see how out of control she had become - no wonder men were terrified of her.

About two weeks before she was due to go home, she met Jed, a landscape architect. They were worlds apart. He spent all his time in nature; she spent all her time in an office. He wanted nothing more than a simple life; she… well, she didn't even know what she wanted anymore.

One night they ended up on the beach, just the two of them. He asked her about her life back home and she told him everything. He didn't seem put off by her success, he seemed impressed. "I can see why you need some time off though," he said, "It sounds like you push yourself too hard! " She felt herself soften every minute she was with him. It was like she could finally relax. She could breathe.

She kept waiting for him to kiss her but when he didn't, she thought "to hell with it," leaned in and kissed him first. He looked surprised but when she pulled away, he pulled her back in.

The next morning he left flowers he'd picked on the pillow next to her, along with a note that said - "Shall we watch the sun set tonight?" It was the most romantic thing she'd ever experienced.

For years, Chloe looked for a man who was even more driven and successful than she was. She looked for someone more Alpha than her, but this never worked out well.

Those guys – Masculine Strength Males – were not that into her. They didn't want competition; they wanted someone to care for them, someone to have fun with—in other words, they wanted someone with a lot of feminine energy, which Chloe was not showing—at all.

Chloe was treating dates like business meetings. She was basically saying, "Here's what I bring to the table, what about you?" There was no room for spontaneity or romance. She'd ditch guys before she ever got a chance to know them properly.

The right match for her is a Feminine Strength Male but she dismissed them because most of the ones she met weren't financially successful or confident enough. But there is more to life than financial success. And just because the Feminine Strength Guys are slower in making the moves, doesn't mean they don't feel passion.

Chloe was used to doing everything on a timetable but love doesn't work like that. The Feminine Strength Males like to move slowly; they are not in a rush—especially for sex.

Taking time off work changed everything for Chloe. For the first time in years, she relaxed. She let go of her masculine need to control and push. She gave up and allowed her feminine energy to take over—which meant she surrendered her control and went with the flow,

It was then that she met someone that she didn't expect to meet. He was gentle, romantic and not materially successful in the way that she was. Because she was on holiday, the relationship had time to blossom. She used her feminine energy to be open-minded and vulnerable with him. She also used her masculine energy to make the first move.

Some women, even Masculine Strength Women, think that the man has to be in charge—but he doesn't. A Feminine Strength Male will love it when you take control; that really turns him on.

You don't have to ask him out, or kiss him, but you have to make it really clear you're interested in him before the Feminine Strength Male will gather the confidence to go for it.

Once you make the first move he can take it from there. Notice that Jed left flowers for her the next day and arranged their next date. And when you date a balanced Feminine Strength Male, he won't be intimidated by your success. He'll love it. Masculine Strength Men would see your success as competition, and very inse-cure Feminine Strength Males might be intimidated. But a guy who is balanced will be proud of his intelligent, feisty, successful girlfriend. He'll love to support you and feel excited to be around your energy.

Chloe's biggest challenge was to accept his love and tenderness—to be vulnerable and open. It was terrifying but exciting.

Can you relate?

Do you want to sort out your love life in the quick and efficient way you do the rest of your life? Have you been accused of intimidating men? Are you looking for your Alpha match? You might think that you want someone just like you, but I warn you that this might not be the best route. It'll result in a clash of egos and a constant power struggle.

Your Bingo Partner

You need a balanced Feminine Strength Male who is gentle, supportive and loving. Someone who offers you things that money can't. Someone who will find your confidence a turn on—not a threat.

How To Get It

BE PATIENT

Masculine Strength Females like quick, logical solutions to solve their problems. They want to find the right guy right now, and get frustrated when it's not happening.

They like to be in control. But when it comes to love, there are no shortcuts. You have to be patient, open and trusting. As they say, love works in mysterious ways. But in order to experience the mystery you have to let go of the idea that you can control everything. This is a challenge, I know.

SLOW DOWN

Masculine Strength Females book their planner up with a different date every night in their quest to find love. They tell themselves it's a numbers game. That's true, to a point, but guys will sense your impatience and the fact that you're just trying to fill a vacancy. This is not a turn-on.

PAMPER YOURSELF

Dress up, do your make-up and hair and get your nails done. You might think that dressing up is a waste of time but it makes a difference in the way you feel about yourself and in the way men respond to you - especially Feminine Strength Males, who are very aesthetic.

MAKE THE FIRST MOVE

Don't be afraid to make the first move. Most Feminine Strength Males lack confidence to approach women first, and will love you for taking charge. If you're in a bar, be the one to strike up conversation. You could compliment a guy on his shirt or ask him what he's drinking. Once you get to know him, you can either be brave and ask him out or drop heavy hints. You can say something like, "Hey, did you hear this movie is playing in theatres?

I really want to go see it," and let him take it from there. I asked my husband Alex out on our first date. I recently asked him if he thought he would have ever asked me out if I hadn't made that first step and he said "Most likely not." Years of joy, fun, love and growth wouldn't have happened if I had not have taken the lead - so be bold. You don't know what it could lead to.

GO ONLINE

As a Masculine Strength Female you can play the online dating game well because you don't over think or take everything personally. It's also much more common for women to take the lead in initiating conversations on-line, so it's a good way for you to play to your strengths.

GIVE MEN A CHANCE

Don't discount a potential mate too quickly just because you didn't like what he said, wore or did on a date. Your masculine energy can make you quick to judge but that's only fear. It's easier to decide someone isn't right or good enough than it is to take a risk. And don't knock a guy just because he doesn't have your level of career success. Balanced Feminine Strength Men are not wimpy fail-ures—far from it. He will offer you things that are more important than money, like emotional support, intima-cy, tenderness and fun, to name a few.

DON'T HIDE YOUR SUCCESS

Masculine Strength Males will feel the need to compete with your success, but Feminine Strength Males will see your confidence and achievements as a huge turn-on. There is nothing more exciting to them than a powerful woman. So don't hide your success on a date. But don't flaunt it either. Love is not a competition in which you need to come out on top.

LET GO OF CONTROL IN BED

Masculine Strength Females can treat sex the way they do every other area of life – with ruthless efficiency. They can jump into bed with a guy and tell them exactly what they want, how they want it and to hurry on. While communication and knowing what you want is great, sometimes it doesn't leave room for softness and romance. You can take the dominant position in bed sometimes, but take it slow initially. Allow your feminine energy partner to show you tenderness and remember that a lot of the masculine need to stay in control comes from fear.

OPEN UP

The hardest thing for the Masculine Strength Females is to open up to other people, express their feelings and allow a relationship to develop. They're terrified of being vulnerable. It's scary to get out of your comfort zone but there's no way around it.

DON'T BE AFRAID TO FALL IN LOVE

You might say, "I'm not afraid to fall in love." But when it happens, the logical mind will most likely want to protect you and make you run away. Falling in love is a very feminine experience and that's why it's so scary for Masculine Strength Males and Females. You have to let go of the mind and let your heart take over. Nobody falls in love logically.

KEEP USING YOUR FEMININE ENERGY

Even when you're in a happy, healthy relationship, continue to nurture and balance both your masculine and feminine energies. Remember that nobody else can make you whole; you need to do that yourself. When you first meet the right guy it will be tempting to give up working on yourself. You'll think that he's the answer to all your problems. He's not. It's important that you keep working on yourself in order to have a happy relationship and a happy life.

192

CHAPTER XV

DATING TIPS FOR THE MASCULINE STRENGTH MALE

WHAT I DIDN'T TELL YOU about Andrew was just how much his ex-girlfriend broke his heart. When he bumped into her at the wedding, it brought it all back to him.

He dated Celia for three years at college. He still remembers the first day he saw her in the library, laughing with a friend. She was beautiful. She was so alive. He went up to her and started talking to her – he can't even remember what they talked about – but he asked her to go out for coffee.

When they dated she drove him nuts. He was infuriated by the amount of time she spent getting ready to go out, the way she changed her mind about everything and her unpredictable moods, but she was the only woman he ever loved. Physically she was exactly what he liked – she had curves, something to hold on to. The sex was amazing. They couldn't get enough of each other, so they spent whole weekends in bed.

But they argued a lot; he couldn't shake the feeling that she might cheat on him. He saw her talk to other guys and he felt a pit of rage in his stomach. It didn't matter how many times she said she'd never cheat – he didn't believe her. In the end she said she couldn't take it anymore. It was over. She couldn't be with someone so jealous and possessive.

After that, Andrew closed down. He slept around a lot and had ten one-night stands in two months. He dated a couple of girls but not for long. They were fit, lean and ambitious; female versions of him. Those relationships never went anywhere so he stuck to online hook - ups— easy, no expectations, but totally empty.

After bumping into his ex at the wedding, Andrew decided to take a break from dating. And from sex. He realized that he needed to sort himself out if he really wanted to get into a serious relationship. And he realized that he really did want that – he wanted marriage and kids and the whole nine yards.

For a year he was celibate as he worked on balancing himself. His friends couldn't believe it. At the same time he started to pay more attention to his grooming. Not that he became a dandy, but he simply put more effort into his appearance.

As he started to slow down, Andrew discovered that he could have conversations with women without feeling that he had to go to bed with them. Before, whenever he hung out with women, he thought, "Am I going to sleep with her?" Now it was different. His female friends saw the change and started introducing him to their friends.

He went on a few set ups. His female friends advised him not to sleep with a woman on the first or second date, or even the third date. It was hard as hell for him but he did it.

Then one day he bumped into a friend's sister, Maia. They started chatting.

"You seem different," she said. He laughed and told her a bit about what had been going on. They went out for coffee. "I always thought you were an asshole," she said. He laughed. He liked her. She was honest, free-spirited and alive.

He asked Maia out again and she said yes. They didn't sleep together for two months. She was testing him, he thought – and he was willing to do whatever it took.

Six months later, nothing about Maia made sense to him. She was chaotic, emotional and unpredictable – and that's what he loved about her.

The unbalanced Masculine Strength Male uses sex as a way to get close to women. There's no romance, no vulnerability and no intimacy. It's just sealing the deal. But as much as he pretends to the outside world that sex is all he wants, it isn't.

Being a playboy can be fun for a while but by the time you're in your thirties it can start to feel empty. He dated Masculine Strength Females because he could relate to them easily – they were like him. And there were no messy emotions.

But that got empty too.

Andrew was ready for something more.

He had to try a whole new approach.

Being celibate was a big thing for him. It taught him how to slow down and open up. He no longer treated every interaction with a woman as a potential gateway to sex. It was a revelation. He could actually talk to women without trying to bed them. Who knew?

Then, when he started dating again, he took the time to really get to know the woman he dated. And even if it didn't end up in sex that was OK.

Andrew used to be scared of the feminine energy—of how unpredictable and sometimes irrational it can be. But once he started to embrace it in himself, he could accept it in others. Then Maia came along – soft, playful, vulnerable and feminine. His Bingo!

Can you relate?

Have you slept around as a way to avoid intimacy? Do you find most women to be unpredictable, irrational and infuriating? Do you find it easier to date girls who are more logical like you? Well, it's time to change your approach. Believe it or not, the infuriating women are the best ones for you.

Your Bingo Partner:

You need a Feminine Strength Female who radiates love, caring and compassion. Someone with curves and softness.

How To Get It

ADMIT YOU WANT TO FIND LOVE

You know you want to find love, even though you have a

hard time admitting it. The fact that you're reading this book is already a huge sign that you're ready to become more balanced. I applaud you for getting over your skepticism and getting this far. That shows that you're already exercising your feminine energy by being open minded and accepting new information. For you, balance and acceptance of the feminine energy within you is the key to finding love and getting in a healthy, long-term relationship.

LOOK AFTER YOUR APPEARANCE

Start with cleaning up yourself physically. It will make you feel good to use your feminine energy to pamper yourself regularly. Dress up, get regular haircuts, shave, groom your nails and toes. If all you own is t-shirts and jeans, please go shopping. Get a personal shopper, or ask a style-savvy friend to assist you.

CLEAN UP

Next, clean up your house. If you don't want to do it, get a cleaner. If you want a woman to feel comfortable in your space you need to show that you care about it. A living room strewn with coffee cups, cereal bowls and takeaway containers will not cut it when you bring a serious date home. Women notice the books on your shelves, the cushions on your sofa and whether or not you have matching bed linen. It will make you feel good to use your feminine energy in order to create a home, rather than a crash pad. It's a sign of maturity.

STOP SLEEPING AROUND

Stop using women for sex. Meaningless sex is fun at first but when you have too much of it, it becomes dull. It's like fast food—empty calories and zero nutritional value. Sex is important in any relationship but it can wait. The best relationships are built on friendship. Get to know her first and let her get to know you. Build anticipation and desire. Believe me, if you wait for it, the sex will be even better because it will be more meaningful.

BE NICE

If you like a woman, be nice to her. Give her a compliment. Ask her questions and listen to her answers without judgment. Show interest in her. Respect her opinions. Masculine Strength Males can mask their insecurities by teasing the women they date and being sarcastic. This is a big no-no. Sure, it's great to use your humor, but make sure it's not at her expense. An unbalanced Masculine Strength Guy will belittle the feminine energy because he feels threatened by it. This is not the way to a woman's heart. Here is where you can exercise your feminine energy: learn to be more sweet and romantic with women. Take your potential mate to a nice restaurant. Make the effort to look nice for your date. You will feel great, and she will appreciate it.

EXPRESS

Once you're in a relationship, don't let your ego get in the way. Express your love verbally and physically by using your feminine energy. Give your partner a hug every time you see her. Tell her that you love her. Send her texts throughout the day to remind her how much you appreciate her in your life.

BE OPEN-MINDED

As a Masculine Strength Male, your Bingo relationship is going to be someone with a feminine energy. The more balanced you are, the better able you are to accept the feminine energy in your partner because you've already accepted it in yourself. But while you're still working on balancing yourself, be patient. Feminine Strength People see the world entirely differently from the way you see it. They might not seem logical or make sense to you, but that's OK. Even if you don't understand the feminine energy, accept it. Embrace it. It's what will make you happy.

KEEP USING YOUR FEMININE ENERGY

Even when you're in a happy, healthy relationship, continue to nurture and balance both your masculine and feminine energies. Remember that nobody else can make you whole. You need to do that yourself. When you first meet the right girl, it will be tempting to give up working on yourself. You'll think that she's the answer to all your problems. She's not. It's important that you keep working on yourself in order to have a happy relationship and a happy life.

BALANCING EXISTING
RELATIONSHIPS

Now we move on to learning how to balance a relationship that you're already in. Although this chapter is focused on romantic relationships in mind, the same advice can apply to any kind of relationship—whether it is with a family member, a co-worker, or a friend, etc. That's the beauty of understanding the masculine and feminine energies – the dynamics between the energies work the same way in any given relationship.

It's likely that you already have a strong sense of what energy your partner has. Is it the opposite energy to the one you have or the same? How do think your energies play out in your relationship?

In this section we'll go through each of the energy combinations and talk you through the strengths and the challenges each combination has. In my experience partners with the same energies have to work harder to balance their relationship, but it can be done.

People in relationships with their opposites will have

a strong attraction, and often their relationship will be more effortless – but there are areas they need to watch out for too.

So, let's get started.

CHAPTER XVI

CHEMISTRY: THE FEMININE STRENGTH FEMALE AND THE MASCULINE STRENGTH MALE

THE BEST PLACE TO START is, with what many people think of as the traditional relationship – between a man with stronger masculine energy and a woman with stronger feminine energy.

Remember my friend, Selina, the one who kept dating sweet but unsuitable guys? Well, let me tell you what happened after she decided to end it with the perfect-on-paper but super-Feminine Strength Male.

A few months after she called it off with the feminine Strength Male she was at a club where she met a guy at the bar. His name was Jack and he wore a bad t-shirt and jeans. He was chunky and swarthy. He wasn't the kind of guy she usually went for but nevertheless she felt attracted to him. He was sure of himself and strong.

He bought her a drink and within ten minutes he asked her out. The next day he came to pick her up on a motorcycle and took her to a hockey match. Who takes a girl to a hockey match on the first date? But she loved it.

The next night they went out again, this time for dinner.

That night they had sex and ended up in bed all weekend. The sex was great. Really great. After that weekend, they were an item. Six months later they got married, and recently they had their first child.

Selina's life is unrecognizable since being with Jack. She's driving his truck. The girl who used to color-code her books is now living in a building site as they renovate their home. It's challenging with a one-year-old baby, but she loves that too. She feels grounded and stronger.

Jack is happy too. Since being with Selina, he's more conscious about what he eats, he goes to the gym and he's taking better care of his body. Before, he just wore jeans and a t-shirt. Now Selina helped Jack get a whole simple but stylish wardrobe.

He loves coming home to her and he loves the kind of mother she is.

It was tough at first. They fought a lot – usually about tiny stuff. She got mad at him for leaving stuff around the house and he couldn't understand why she lost it over a pair of shoes on the carpet. It's just a pair of shoes!

She thought he was acting like a pig and he thought she was over-reacting. A huge fight came out of nothing. And it didn't help that Selina wouldn't let things lie. She wanted to talk about problems endlessly but Jack needed space to calm down. A few times he walked out of the house; otherwise they would end up in a fight and say things they later regretted.

With time though, they're getting better at communicating. Selina is learning to express herself more calmly and she picks her moments. She tries not to attack. And she gives him space when he comes home from work.

For his part Jack is gradually learning to open up to Selina. And put away his shoes.

The physical attraction between Masculine Strength Males and Feminine Strength Females is magnetic. Sex is very important to both sides. They can spend days in bed. It's a huge part of the relationship.

Masculine Strength Males love soft, feminine curves and Feminine Strength Females get hugely turned on by a sturdy guy with strong hands and an angular jaw.

It works beyond the physical level too.

Jack grounds Selina. When she talks about something he brings a completely different point of view. This helps her to see the world in a different way. And just being with him makes her feel calmer. He encourages her to be more independent, adventurous and decisive.

And Selina helps Jack to open up. She's learning that she needs to give him time and space. She needs to encourage Jack to talk by asking gentle questions at the right time. She's working on listening more, asking questions and giving him time to open up.

He's a lot more stylish now, because she goes shopping with him. She's taught him that image is very important. He has his own business and impressions count.

There can be clashes. Selina likes the finer things in life and Jack can't understand where the money goes. But deep down Jack wants Selina to have everything she wants.

And so it goes with the modern relationship between the Feminine Strength Female and the Masculine Strength Male. Their differences create the spark, but they both work on balancing themselves and compromising. They respect each other and learn together.

This is not always the case. Without balance and compromise, the combination of opposites can be an explosive one. Take Greg and Anne, a couple who has been married for thirty years. Like Selina and Jack, the sexual attraction was always there, but it came at a price.

The Unbalanced Masculine and Feminine Energy Relationship

Greg and Anne met on a bus thirty years ago. She was a 19-year-old student and he was a 25-year-old waiter with dreams of owning his own restaurant. Greg moved quickly. He told her that she was the most beautiful woman he'd ever seen and that he wanted to marry her.

Anne was embarrassed and thrilled. They got off the bus and had coffee. Within six weeks they were married. The sex was always inventive and passionate. He was her first love and while he'd had girlfriends before, he told her that she was the only woman he had ever met that he wanted to spend the rest of his life with.

Within three months Anne was pregnant. Over the next five years they had three more children. Money was tight and they lived with his parents for the first two years of their marriage. He worked long hours and when he came home, he had a temper. He loved the children but he didn't show it. He shouted at them to stay quiet.

The angrier and more aggressive Greg became, the more emotional and passive Anne became. She didn't know how to stand up for herself or how to stand up to him.

When they argued she would become upset and start crying; she became too upset to communicate properly. She talked around and around in circles, her voice getting higher and higher. Greg couldn't stand it when Anne cried. It killed him. He felt like a failure.

Soon he stopped coming home straight after work. She found out that he was cheating on her, and they fought even more.

Anne wanted to leave but they had children and she couldn't afford to raise them on her own. She only worked part-time. Greg was the main bread winner and that gave him all the power.

Anne's only way of retaliating was with silence. Whole weeks went by when she wouldn't speak to Greg. Sometimes after a fight she wrote him a letter—that was the only way she felt she could express herself. Eventually they would make up with passionate sex. Things would be fine for a while until there was another explosive row.

Greg didn't like Anne to go out without him because he was sure she was flirting with men. Twenty years into their marriage, the sex is the only good thing to remain. They still don't know how to talk to each other.

This is a classic example of what happens when you put an unbalanced Masculine Strength Male together with an unbalanced Feminine Strength Female. The fact that they are opposites is what makes the attraction electric—but they may as well be from different worlds.

Greg couldn't handle how emotional his wife was. It killed him when she cried – it made him feel like a failure. As a man, he felt it was his job to keep her happy and he obviously wasn't doing that. He didn't realize that the feminine energy likes to cry and express, it's their form of release.

All Anne wanted was for Greg to be there for her, to hold her and listen sympathetically. Instead he got angry. And the more aggressive he became, the more submissive she became.

It was a downward spiral. Greg felt like such a failure at home that he stayed away and started having affairs. And to add insult to injury, he then accused Anne of flirting with other guys. He became controlling, jealous, possessive and paranoid.

For many years it was a mess. Because Greg did not work on expressing his own sensitive, emotional, feminine energy, he could not tolerate it in Anne. He despised her weakness.

And because Anne had not developed her own strong, assertive, powerful masculine energy, she couldn't match his. She couldn't stand up for herself or her children.

The good news is that even this kind of relationship can be rescued if both people simply learn to balance their energies.

After Greg and Anne's children left home for college, they realized they couldn't continue to live the way they were. They talked about divorce but neither of them wanted to end it. They loved each other; they just didn't know how to talk to each other.

Anne decided to go back to work full-time. Having financial independence made Anne feel stronger. She knew in the back of her mind that if she had to leave, she could.

Previously she would do anything to avoid an argument because she hated conflict. Increasingly though, she found herself answering back when Greg was rude and unkind. She practiced keeping her voice low when she spoke and she used her body language to stand more solidly. In this way she learned to use her masculine energy. And far from causing problems, Greg liked her more when she started to respect herself.

For years Greg dictated their social life—or lack of one. He was never interested in going out. Now, however, if there was something she wanted to attend – a party or a wedding – she went on her own if Greg did not want to go. And the more she went out on her own, the more Greg missed her. "Can I come with you?" he asked one day when she was going to a work BBQ. "If you like," she said and smiled. The balance had shifted.

How to Balance This Relationship

The most important thing is that you must both learn to embrace your differences. Masculine and Feminine Strength People see the world differently. This is what attracts them to each other but it's also what challenges them, making it the perfect learning opportunity. Instead of fighting, learn from each other and help each other grow and balance. Relationships are like a mirror – they show us what we need to learn.

Tips for the Feminine Strength Female

WRITE A LETTER

For the Feminine Strength Female, it can be hard to express yourself without getting overcome with emotions. This is something the masculine energy finds hard to handle. It can cause fights to escalate without getting anything resolved. If you recognize this, try writing letters to your partner. It can be easier to express yourself logically and calmly on paper when you are on your own and have time to think.

WRITE A JOURNAL

Keeping a journal also helps. When you write down how you feel it's a release. It can also help you to understand your emotions instead of getting overwhelmed by them. That will help you communicate with your partner more calmly and effectively.

GIVE HIM SPACE

The Masculine Strength Male needs to switch off at the end of the day. He needs quiet time so that he can retreat and recharge. The Feminine Strength Female is the opposite; she wants to talk everything through. You can talk but you have to pick your moments and give him the space he needs first.

ENCOURAGE HIM TO OPEN UP

Ask very specific but gentle questions in order to encourage the masculine energy to express. Once he does start sharing, don't interrupt him.

DON'T NAG

It might drive you crazy that he leaves coffee cups everywhere or that there are wet towels in the bathroom but nagging him won't help. He'll feel criticized and attacked and will either get angry or retreat. It's much more effective to use positive reinforcement. Admire him and praise him when he makes the effort. Tell him how grateful you are that he emptied the dishwasher or brought out the trash. He will do it more.

COMMUNICATE

The Masculine Strength Male wants his partner to be happy; he wants to provide for her and protect her. When she's unhappy he takes it personally. He feels like he is failing. When you are upset, explain to him that you just need to talk, and that you aren't blaming him. Tell him that you need his support, and he'll be there for you.

TRUST HIM

When the Masculine Strength Male has a problem, he goes away on his own until he can find a way to fix it. If you offer advice when he hasn't asked for it, he might think that you're saying that he's not capable of dealing with the situation himself. Instead, tell him that you have complete faith in his ability to solve the problem. Tell him that you trust him. Let him take charge and make decisions.

STAND UP FOR YOURSELF

The Feminine Strength Female is inclined to let small things slide in order to have a quiet life. The feminine energy hates confrontation. But this doesn't work in the long run. All the unsaid things build up during a relationship and this causes resentment which usually surfaces at an inappropriate time and way. Learn to stand up for yourself even when it comes to tiny things—like a partner who leaves a mess or is always late. Try practicing with your friends if you like. Your partner will respect you more for it, and believe me—taking a stand will give you a feeling of strength and power that will affect every area of your life.

GIVE MASSAGES

Give him a foot rub on the sofa or a shoulder massage. Small acts of affection will make him feel connected to you and appreciated.

KEEP THE SPARK ALIVE

Strong physical attraction is something you two have in spades. But even in this relationship, work, children and a busy life can take its toll on your love life. Make time to make love. It's hugely important to both of you but especially the Masculine Strength Male, who sees sex as a way of showing you his love. If you're not in the mood he takes it as a personal rejection.

Tips for the Masculine Strength Male

LEARN TO LISTEN

When The Masculine Strength Male talks, he wants to get to the point. When the Feminine Strength Female talks, she does so to express her feelings and connect with others. She doesn't want you to solve her problems. She just wants your sympathy and understanding. So even if it drives you crazy, listen to her. Give her attention and time. Be understanding when someone upsets her. Do not judge her as weak for her need for reassurance. You will become closer if you can be there for her in this way. You will be her rock.

LET HER CRY

It's awful to see the woman you love upset, but her tears are not a reflection on you. You're not a failure because your loved one is crying. For the Feminine Strength Female tears are a healthy release. It makes her feel better. Don't run away or get angry. Sit with her. Support her. Hug her.

EXPRESS

Your big challenge is to open up and share what you feel more. You might not even know what it is you feel but you do have feelings, it's just that society has told you that feelings are a sign of weakness so you've suppressed them. Getting over this will not come easily to you but you don't need to spend hours talking about your feelings. Just share something. Speak about your fears. Trust that she will be there for you.

BE MORE ROMANTIC

Call her from work to tell her you love her. Book a table at her favorite restaurant. Come home with flowers. These small, romantic gestures will make her feel loved and cherished. Encourage her to treat herself. Tell her that she deserves that new dress or that she should go out and get a massage.

SHOW AFFECTION

As a Masculine Strength Male you need to start hugging, kissing and touching your partner more often. Not only as a prelude to sex—but also as a way of showing her you care. Learn to practice day to day affection. Start by giving her a hug when you leave and when you come home. Make plans to leave her sweet notes or send her sexy texts throughout the day. Let her know how hot you find her.

GIVE HER A COMPLIMENTS

Masculine Strength Males are not big talkers so compliments don't come naturally. You might wonder why you need to tell her she looks pretty. You might think she should already know you find her beautiful. But there is a point. It's amazing to watch a woman melt when you offer a sincere compliment from your heart. A simple "I love your eyes" can work miracles.

SHOW APPRECIATION

Feminine Strength Females need praise. Show that you appreciate the little things your partner does and thank her for them. Don't take her for granted.

17

BALANCE: THE FEMININE STRENGTH MALE AND MASCULINE STRENGTH FEMALE

THIS BRINGS ME to another kind of relationship, one that is increasingly common in today's world, and one that I am in with my husband, Alex - a Masculine Strength Female and a Feminine Strength Male.

Later I will share more about my relationship but at this point I'd like to tell you about Gemma and Simon.

Gemma was attracted to Simon the first time she saw him. She was at a friend's birthday party and he was in the kitchen making drinks. He was tall, good-looking and well-dressed. He was smiling and talking to everyone. He was confident and seemed fun. Gemma went straight up to him. "So are you going to make me a cocktail then?" she asked him.

Her friends laughed at how obvious she was, but Gemma always went after what she wanted. She was pretty and confident; she didn't see the point in messing around. For the rest of the party, she didn't leave his side. She thought they had fun but she was annoyed that he didn't make a move at the end of the night. Didn't he like her?

The next day she called up the birthday girl and asked her friend to pass on her number. He called a week later and they went out to a hip bar where Simon seemed to know everybody. It turned out that Simon was a part-time DJ there. In Gemma's mind he was getting cooler by the minute.

They danced all night and he made her laugh. They had fun.

Five years and two children later they are still having fun, but Gemma sometimes wonders if fun is enough.

Soon after she began dating Simon, she realized that he didn't earn a lot of money. Gemma had spent her twenties working ferociously hard at a marketing company. Simon, on the other hand, spent those years working in bars and travelling. Gemma saved hard and was able to buy her first property when she was 25. Simon had never owned his own place. When they first met, that didn't matter. She loved how fun and free-spirited he was. He made her lighten up and do things she'd never do—but now that they had a family, the financial pressures were showing.

Simon made a huge effort to become financially re-sponsible once they got together. He quit the DJ gig and worked at the bar full-time. He made his way up to man-ager and then became the manager of a chain of bars. With both their salaries they earned a good living, but for Gemma it wasn't enough. She wished he was more successful. She was fed up of being the main earner. Si-mon didn't understand why she wasn't happy with what they had. In his eyes it was already more than most.

Now Simon wants to start his own bar, but Gemma tells him they can't take the risk financially. Simon knows there's a risk, but he feels sure that if she would help him they could do it. He wishes Gemma would have more faith in him. He finds it demoralizing when he tries to be more of the man she wants him to be, and yet she continues to put him down. She doesn't even seem to want him to touch her any more. It's not that he wants sex all the time, but he feels rejected when she always says no. Worse than that, he feels emasculated.

Gemma doesn't mean to make Simon feel this way. It's just hard to muster up the energy and desire for sex when she's juggling a big job, a house and two kids. When they do have sex, she just wants to get the job done—to have an orgasm and move on. She loves Simon. She loves how kind, sweet and patient he is with the kids. She loves how he cooks her dinners and always buys her imaginative presents and leaves her little notes. She loves that he's happy to change diapers and get up in the night. But sometimes she gets resentful of him. She wishes he was more of a provider; she wishes she didn't always have to be the boss.

Gemma and Simon's relationship is increasingly common these days – it's often referred to as the relationship between an Alpha female and a Beta male.

Historically, men were the breadwinners and women suppressed their ambitions to support their man in his career. That's no longer the case. Today, Masculine Strength Women can use their natural confidence, assertiveness and ambition to excel in every area of life. Meanwhile, Feminine Strength Men are allowed to embrace their natural gifts, such as their kindness, creativity, and ability to communicate.

It sounds like the perfect, modern, union. And in lots of ways it is.

Gemma and Simon have so much going for them. She brings the masculine drive and ambition. He brings the feminine fun and lightness. He's a wonderful, hands-on father who makes her stop and relax when she's doing too much.

But there are challenges too.

At first, Gemma loved that Simon was fun and spontaneous, but she's come to disrespect him for his lack of ambition. Likewise, easy-going Simon was turned on by Gemma's energy and drive when they met but he has come to feel disempowered by it after five years together.

To make this union work, they need to meet in the middle. They each need to balance their masculine and feminine energies.

Until Gemma learns to embrace her own free-spirited feminine energy, she will resent that energy in Simon. Until Simon learns to take charge and stand up for himself by using his masculine energy, he is going to resent Gemma's strength.

Gemma says she wants Simon to take charge but the truth is that she doesn't let him. He's already stepped up by working harder and becoming more successful, but now that he wants to take the next step and open his own business she doesn't trust him enough to help him do it.

Her masculine energy makes her cynical and judgmental. She says she wants someone else to take control but she holds on tight to the reigns. She still wants to be the one in charge. She doesn't trust him to be the leader. And how does that make Simon feel? It makes him feel like a child. A lot of Feminine Strength Males feel this way because their partner does not allow them to be the boss at least sometimes.

The best thing for Gemma to do right now is to encourage Simon. He just wants to hear that she believes in him—then he can fly.

When Gemma encourages Simon, she uses her masculine strength—because she's being his rock—but she also uses her feminine energy of caring, trusting and encouraging. She needs to be softer, kinder and more accepting. When she becomes more feminine, he will have no choice but to step up his game and take the next step.

But Gemma must remember something else. She needs to hold on to the reason she fell in love with Simon in the first place. She loved his playfulness, his joy, his sweet and loving character. If Gemma married someone as driven as her, would they ever see the children? Would they ever have the same amount of fun?

Gemma has to remember that life is about much more than money and success. It's about love and family and enjoying the small moments.

Simon also needs to step up to the plate. He needs to take responsibility for his end of the finances. He needs to learn how to bring his dreams to life instead of living in a dream world. In other words, he needs to embrace his masculine energy. And the more he does this, the less Gemma will feel like she's with a boy and therefore treat him that way.

How to Balance This Relationship

OWN YOUR STRENGTHS

There's a good chance that the Masculine Strength Female will be the main breadwinner in the relationship. This is not something to be ashamed of or to apologize for. Take pride in your success and in your ability to contribute to the family's well-being. The Feminine Strength Male also needs to own his strengths. You bring warmth and fun to the relationship. You work but you're not a workaholic. You support your partner in her goals. You're secure enough in yourself to not be threatened by her strength. You're a wonderful, present parent.

BALANCE YOURSELF FIRST

If both partners stay set in their masculine and feminine roles, there's a good chance that they will resent each other further down the line. The Masculine Strength Female has to learn to relax, trust and have faith in her partner. She has to learn to let go of control—at least some of the time—otherwise she will emasculate him. Likewise, the Feminine Strength Male has to take charge on occasion by using his masculine energy. He can't be afraid to push back when she's controlling. He needs to speak up and stand up for himself in this relationship, otherwise his Masculine Strength Female will slowly lose respect for him.

SHARE THE CHORES

If you're a Masculine Strength Female and you're the

main breadwinner, do not be afraid to ask your partner to take on a greater share of childcare or housework. Many women have tried to do it all and then became resentful. That doesn't help anybody. And the chances are that your partner will love being more involved at home. It's playing to his strengths and he will gain power from feeling useful and important.

DISCUSS MONEY OPENLY

Money can end up being a big issue in this partnership. As difficult as it is, you need to discuss finances honestly. Both sides need to say what they can provide and what they expect. The masculine energy often wants more money, status, and property while the feminine energy is happy with less. What kind of compromise can you come to?

SWAP ROLES IN BED

A lot of Masculine Strength Females have big jobs and are in control of every aspect of their lives; the bedroom can be a good place to let go of that role. If the Feminine Strength Male can take the lead when it comes to sex, it will bring out his masculine energy and her feminine energy. Also, wearing some sexy lingerie will help the Masculine Strength Female bring out her feminine energy. Believe me, your Feminine Strength Male will appreciate it, as he is highly aesthetic.

SLOW DOWN IN BED

Many Masculine Strength Females see sex as a means

to and end; they want to have the orgasm and skip fore-play. This is the exact opposite of how the Feminine Strength Male approaches sex. He wants to take it slow and make love. The Masculine Strength Female needs to slow down and embrace the intimacy and sensuality of foreplay. Try introducing massages, stroking and kissing before you have sex. And before you make any excuses, yes, you do have time.

DO NOT LISTEN TO OTHER PEOPLE'S OPINIONS

Masculine Strength Females and Feminine Strength Males make wonderful partners, but they don't fit into the traditional model of a relationship. Some people will wonder why—as a bright and successful woman—you don't find someone as successful as you. They don't see that your partner provides emotional and practical support that allows you to be yourself. The Feminine Strength Male is emotionally open, respectful and nurturing. Far from being someone you settle for, he's a catch—and don't let anyone tell you otherwise.

CHAPTER XVIII

50:50 PARTNERS: THE MASCULINE-MASCULINE RELATIONSHIP

WHEN TWO MASCULINE STRENGTH People are in a relationship they are commonly referred to as two Alphas. Now, how do you think this partnership goes? Is it all smiles and roses? Well, not really. But they do make for a formidable partnership.

Ed has a name for his wife, Nicki: The General. What she says goes. It's always done. He was dating someone else when they met and so was Nicki but that didn't matter. Nicki gave Ed her number, flirted outrageously, and soon they were together.

A couple of years after they met, Nicki proposed to him. She was 27 and wanted to get married and have kids. She told him that if he didn't want to get married, she didn't want to waste her time, she'd go find someone else.

It was not the most romantic marriage proposal, but it was effective. They went shopping that day and bought cheap rings, she spent $100 on a dress, and they got married a month later in a small ceremony with a few friends and family. There was no fuss.

They've now been married ten years and have two sons together. They're a team, a great partnership. They split the chores 50-50 and their house runs like clockwork. Ed runs two successful online businesses and Nicki is a personal trainer. Every Sunday night they sit down and plan the upcoming week together so that everything that needs to get done gets done.

They live in a big house in a lovely neighborhood. Nicki doesn't need to work for financial reasons but she can't imagine giving up her career.

Early in the marriage Ed was unfaithful. He always had a high sex drive and after the kids Nicki didn't have the energy or inclination to make love. To be honest, the cheating didn't bother her that much. As long as he kept being a great dad and a partner she could live with it.

And Ed is a great father. He hugs the children all the time, reads to them and picks them up from school. He shows a tender side with the children that she never saw in him before.

Ed wishes he could show this side to Nicki. Sometimes he wishes she was the kind of woman who wanted to be looked after, but she's not. She's too strong and independent for that. Whenever he tries to do something romantic for her, like bring her flowers, she makes fun of him. "What have you done?!" she asks sarcastically. He hasn't done anything. He gives up.

Nicki knows that she's not very emotional or romantic with her husband. Sometimes she wishes they did more things together, like go dancing, but Ed isn't very interested.

In many ways, a partnership between two Masculine Strength People really works. Both are confident, strong and goal-oriented. Together they can get anything done and their lives function well. They work as a team. There are systems and rules in place so everything goes smoothly. There's a plan for everything. Everybody knows what to do and when.

Masculine Strength People are drawn to each other because they understand each other. It's their similarities that cause the problems.

They often butt heads because they both want to be the boss. There's a clash of egos. The challenge is exciting at first but after a while, one of the two gets tired of competing. Relationships are a dance. But in this dance there is no leader and no follower, there are two people trying to lead.

One of the biggest struggles for Masculine Strength People is being able to express their emotions, so this relationship can be more like a business partnership than a great romance.

Feminine Strength People, with all their feelings and changing moods, might confuse the hell out of them, but they also offer them a lot of what they need because they both lack the same thing— the caring, soft, loving touch; the expressive, emotional, feminine energy.

Neither one of them is naturally romantic. Both can be cynical.

Sex can become an issue. For the Masculine Strength Male sex is very important. He wants a lot of it. It's his way of showing affection. This can cause problems because the Masculine Strength Female doesn't have the same level of high sex drive.

She is more practical. She likes to work first and play later. She's very goal-oriented and wants to get things done. That doesn't mean she's not sexual. It just means she doesn't need to do it every day. Once or twice a week is more than enough.

For this reason, infidelity is often an issue in this kind of relationship. He cheats because he wants sex and attention, and then she sleeps with someone else as retaliation. Or she might accept his sexual infidelity as long as he's loyal to the family. Or, she can work on her feminine sexual energy.

For this relationship to blossom both of the partners need to bring out their feminine energy.

Children can help bring out the loving and nurturing feminine energy. After middle age men's testosterone levels drop and this also makes them balance more and be more inclined to stay at home and spend time with the family.

Another challenge is learning to take turns being the boss. When one partner excels in a certain area, the other can sit back and let them take the lead. You can flip-flop from relax-mode to in-charge mode. It takes work on both sides to be romantic and gentle with each other—to remember that this is love, not just a partnership.

How to Balance This Relationship

SHARE DECISIONS

First things first: stop the power struggle. Learn to share

the decisions in your relationship. Remember that you're equal partners. There is no boss in this relationship. You can decide that one partner makes the decisions in one area of your life while other partner takes care of other areas. Or you can sit down and discuss all the decisions as matters arise. Avoid making decisions without your partner and assuming you have the final say—unless it is an area where you have both decided you have that authority. Be inclusive.

UNDERSTAND EACH OTHER'S POSITION

One of the main challenges for the masculine energy is to express feelings and empathize with other people's emotions. Because of this, a conversation can turn into a game of point scoring or a debate. Work on hearing the other person's point of view, and try to understand their position even if you don't agree with it.

SECRET DATE NIGHTS

Take turns organizing "Secret dates." On this night one person organizes everything on the date and the other person says "yes" to it all. On the following date swap roles. This is a great way to share power and control and it can be a lot of fun. It's a great way to use both of your energies. Taking control is a very masculine energy, surrendering is feminine.

MAKE TIME TO TALK

Make time in your day to talk with each other about your day. Even twenty minutes a day before you go to sleep can make a big difference. Schedule it. Masculine Strength People are not great talkers. They can find it hard to express themselves or their emotions. But they have to work on it to keep intimacy.

DO THINGS TOGETHER

The masculine energy loves its independence, so two Masculine Strength People can be like ships in the night. You're both doing your own thing. But for a relationship to work, you need to spend more time together. You need closeness and freedom, independence and interdependence. Sign up for some kind of an activity or a class together. It could be yoga, dancing, painting or anything else you both have interest in.

CUDDLE

Feminine Strength People have a very easy time being affectionate. They like to cuddle and kiss. A Masculine Strength Couple might not have such warmth. Make an effort to show physical affection. This doesn't mean sex. It means taking time to cuddle up on the sofa or rub each other's feet at the end of the day. Make a commitment to kiss each other every morning. Small acts of tenderness will have a huge effect on the warmth in your relationship and will make you feel more connected.

BUY FLOWERS

The feminine energy is usually the one to bring romance to a relationship. The masculine energy is more practical. What's the point of flowers when they're going to die? And who needs candles when you have lights? Trust me, the smell of roses in the air and the dim flicker of candles can make even an ordinary Monday evening feel special. You don't need to do it all the time, but these small feminine touches can keep the romance alive in your relationship

WEAR SEXY UNDERWEAR

The Masculine Strength Female is the kind who wears simple white underwear. She doesn't have time for lace and thongs. But wearing sexy underwear will please your partner. It doesn't have to be all the time, but it's very important to keep the spark alive.

LEAVE LOVE LETTERS

When was the last time you left a little note for your partner? Just a scribble on a piece of paper saying "I love you" left on the kitchen table. Or a text during the day to say "I'm thinking of you" or "Can't wait to see you later." Most people stop flirting when they're in relationships—especially when it's two masculine energies. If you want to have a happy relationship, you must always find ways to show your partner how much you love them.

SWITCH OFF YOUR PHONES

The masculine energy finds it hard to switch off. The masculine energy couple is that couple that sits up in bed and checks e-mails before they fall asleep rather than checking in with each other. This creates a huge distance between them. Once a week set aside time when you don't have your phones with you and you just spend time together. Sunday is usually a good day. It doesn't have to be all day–just a few hours can make a big difference.

DANCE
Dancing is a great way to bring out your feminine energy. It's fluid and expressive and when it's done right it's very sexy. Take dance classes and learn something passionate like Tango, or you can just go dancing together in your local club. It'll bring you both out of your heads and into your bodies.

HIRE A CLEANER
The masculine energy thinks it has better things to do than sweep the floor and that's fine, but if you live in messy house it will drive you crazy. It will also build resentment because privately you are both waiting for the other to take charge of the chores but it isn't happening. Do yourselves a favor and hire a cleaner.

SPEND TIME WITH YOUR CHILDREN
I've seen Masculine Strength Partnerships transform incredibly once children arrive. They bring out a softness in you that you didn't know you had. Make the effort to spend as much time with your children as you can. It will bring out your playful, caring and patient, feminine side.

CHAPTER XIX

FIREWORKS:
THE FEMININE-FEMININE
RELATIONSHIP

Now we come to the fireworks. The Feminine Strength Partnership has the most sparks, the most emotions, and is the hardest combination to make work in the long term.

It's not a lack of love that's the problem. Quite the opposite.

When I met Matt and Celine they seemed incredibly happy together. Then I got to know them better and the truth emerged.

Celine was in a very dark place when she met Matt. She had just ended a bad relationship and was laid off from her marketing job. Her confidence was at an all-time low. When her friend asked her over for a barbeque she said "no" at first but her friend insisted. "You can't stay at home crying forever," she said. So Celine put on a dress and some make up and went out, expecting to be back in a couple of hours.

Then she met Matt. He was open and smiling and they got talking. He told her that he liked her dress. She

said she admired his cool glasses. "Mutual apprecia-
tion!" said Matt. They laughed. He was so easy to talk
to. She found herself telling him all about her aggressive
ex and her horrible job. He listened to her patiently. He
was very understanding.

She had no intention of jumping into another relationship. But they started hanging out—at first as friends—
then slowly it developed into something more. The sex
was beautiful. It was tender and intense. They connected
both physically and emotionally.

Matt always encouraged Celine. When she said it
was her dream to become a nutritionist, he told her she
should do it. "You can do anything you want to do," he
said. She never experienced such love and support from
a man before. He suggested she move in with him to save
money while she got her training.

Celine got a job as a waitress and signed up for a nutritionist course. Matt worked part-time as a sound engineer and tried to make his way as a musician. They
weren't earning big money but it was enough to get by.
Matt was so talented that Celine was sure it was only a
matter of time before he made it big with his music. Until then they had each other.

Four years later, they still loved each other deeply but
they had both changed. Celine had not only qualified as
a nutritionist but through a lot of work she made a name
for herself. Her blog was a popular source of healthy
recipes and she planned to write a book. It was exciting.
She still wasn't making a lot of money, but she hoped
that would come.

There was just one problem. While Celine became successful, Matt still struggled with his music. He came close to a big break a couple of times but nothing happened. He was becoming disheartened. Celine tried to encourage him – she believed so much in his talent – but it was hard.

Celine wanted them to buy their own place but she couldn't see how they could afford it. She already paid more of their rent most months. She didn't want him to give up on his dreams. But she knew that if they wanted to move forward, they both needed to earn more money.

It was hard for them to talk about the real issues, so they ignored them and started fighting over nothing instead. Afterwards they both tried to make it right but nothing ever got resolved. Their sex life was suffering. Celine wasn't turned on by Matt anymore and Matt seemed to have lost any interest in sex. It was like they had become brother and sister, or two roommates. But neither wanted to let go.

Furthermore Celine was waiting for Matt to propose—she felt that would change something—but he hadn't taken that step yet and with things so tense she didn't know if it ever would.

Feminine Strength People are kind, caring and compassionate, so a lack of love is not going to be the problem with this kind of relationship. Because they are both emotionally open, there can be a great connection and amazingly intimate sex. From the outside it looks like the kind of relationship that everybody wants. They are affectionate, supportive and can talk for hours.

The struggle comes further down the line. What the feminine energy wants more than anything is for somebody to take control, and in the Feminine Strength Partnership that doesn't happen. Nobody makes decisions. Nobody makes a plan.

Both are unable to provide what the other needs, which is stability and grounding.

Relationship is like a dance. Someone needs to lead and someone needs to follow. Here there are two followers. Therefore it's easy for this relationship to go nowhere.

They try to solve their problems by endless talking but they never tackle a problem head-on, so nothing gets settled. They're both expressive so matches go up and fire happens. They feel better afterwards but nothing really changes.

Money is often an issue in this relationship. Feminine Strength People have many talents but financial management is not usually one of them. This kind of couple can remain perpetually in a situation where they struggle to make ends meet.

Soon the sex can suffer. While the Feminine Strength Female has a high sex drive, the Feminine Strength Male doesn't. He is happy to have sex and connect this way but he might not take the lead or be as dominant as she'd like him to be. To have sexual attraction you need polarity – you need differences. Over time the lack of polarity can cause a problem, unless one of you plays the more masculine role.

After four years neither of them has committed. Why?

Because the feminine energy is free flowing. If Matt had been with a Masculine Strength Female, she'd be like, "Excuse me, either you put a ring on it, or I'm out." Celine is not so pushy but she's still unsatisfied with the fact that they're drifting.

The only way for this kind of relationship to work is for one or both partners to bring out more of their masculine energy.

Usually it works best if the man in the relationship takes on the more masculine role. Being a man, it's easier for him to do—but it will take an effort. The Feminine Strength Female will find it way too tiresome to take the lead and be the masculine force all the time. This is what Celine is experiencing. She's the one paying most of their rent and making the money but it doesn't make her feel good. It makes her resentful.

Neither person in the relationship is getting what they need but nobody has the courage to break it up or the ability to sort out a plan for how to make things better.

How to Balance This Relationship

VISUALIZE THE FUTURE

Feminine Strength People live in the moment. They don't think about tomorrow or next week, let alone next year. The word plan makes them come out in a sweat. But they're very good at using their intuition and their imagination. As a couple, use this to your advantage. Take a day together to dream about your future. Close your eyes for a few minutes and imagine what your life would be like in a year, in five years – even twenty years from now. Where are you? What are you doing? How do you feel? Now share that image with your partner. Are your visions aligned? Does it feel exciting to share that picture? Make the image as vivid as you can, fill in all the details. Keep going back to that image until it starts to feel real.

PLAN AND SET GOALS

Now that you have your dream picture, it's time for the most important part: break down exactly what it will take to make this vision happen. What steps do you both need to take and when? How are you going to take those steps? Who do you need to call? How much money do you have to earn? What plans do you need to make? Now write these stages down and put them into a calendar. Do it. Actually write it down. When you write things down and schedule them it makes them real.

WEEKLY MEETINGS

Sit down once a week and assess where you are with regards to your plans. Make this time non-negotiable. Pick a time when you know that both of you will be at home. Maybe Sunday night? Make a ritual of it; do it over tea, or before you make dinner together. Light candles, put on music, use your feminine energy to make this time feel special.

GET HELP

Get other people involved in your plans. This will help you to become accountable. Find an accountant or a financial advisor to help you plan your financial future. Get a personal trainer. Both of you will benefit from some hardcore exercise to bring out your masculine energy. Find a tough-love Masculine Strength friend whom you can talk to and count on to always tell you the truth.

DO THINGS INDEPENDENTLY

Feminine Strength People love closeness and intimacy. Masculine Strength People love freedom. In this relationship there might not be enough time spent apart. Make sure that you go out independently—not as a couple--one night a week. When you reunite there will be lots to talk about.

BRING OUT YOUR MASCULINE ENERGY

In order for this relationship to work long term one of you is going to have to step up and develop a lot more masculine energy. Who is that going to be? Is that you? If so, how do you feel about it? If you are a woman, think realistically about whether or not you will be changing yourself too much in order to make this relationship work.

MAKE A DECISION

Break up or commit. The problem with the feminine energy is that it can't make a decision. Two Feminine Strength People can stay in a relationship for a long time simply because neither of them has the courage to break up. On the flipside, neither has the courage to make the commitment it takes to make a relationship work.

CHAPTER XX

THE BINGO RELATIONSHIP
IN ACTION

IN THE LAST FOUR CHAPTERS we explored the dynamics between the masculine and feminine energies in different kinds of couples. Each partnership has its strengths and challenges.

As I've said before, intimate relationships act like a mirror. They reflect back the lessons you need to learn. But everything starts with you. Don't expect the other person to change. It's your job to balance yourself.

It's not always easy, but it's worth it. Relationships are our greatest opportunity, not only for joy but also for growth. What happens when you both work at balancing your energies? You have a Bingo Relationship; the kind I have with my husband Alex.

I remember clearly the moment I started to fall in love with Alex. I worked on Saturdays at a bank where he also worked. One day I had a really bad cough. He wasn't working that day but he came in to the office to pick something up and when he noticed my cough he asked if I was okay.

"Yeah, it's just a cold," I said. I went back to serving customers. About ten minutes later he came back and left a packet of throat lozenges on my desk. He just put them down and said, "See you later."

It was such a tiny gesture but to me it was the sweetest thing. I was doing my very masculine energy thing of just working and pushing through my cold. I didn't see it as such then but he was showing his caring, feminine energy. I didn't know any other guy that would do something so considerate. To this day I tell Alex, "That's how you won my heart—with a pack of Strepsils."

It took me a while to realize that I was attracted to him, though.

Every week I'd look at the schedule to see if we worked the same shifts. I was always disappointed if we weren't—but even then I didn't really realize why I was disappointed.

Meanwhile, Alex kept saying general things to me like, "You should come camping with my friends and I" or " Come out to dinner with my friends and I". But he never followed it up with any firm plans. And I was seeing someone else at the time and he was too, so in my head we were just friends.

One day I suggested that we go ice skating. I didn't have ice skates because money was tight, so I said, "Hey, if you want to go ice skating with me, find me some skates, and I will go with you."

He said, "Done deal!" and borrowed some ice skates from a friend. The next day we went ice-skating. To me, it was two friends, two co-workers going ice-skating. To

Alex, it was a green light; it gave him the confidence to think I was interested. I wasn't even thinking about that, at least not consciously.

So we went ice-skating, which was cute because he wasn't very good at it, which gave him the chance to hug and hold on to me. Still, in my head, we were friends. After the ice-skating he said, "Let's have dinner." I thought, "Oh no ... this is starting to sound like a date."

I said that I wasn't really hungry but he persisted and we went for sushi.

The second time we went out—again, as friends so far as I was concerned—he kissed me. I freaked out! I didn't say anything. I just backed away. In my mind this wasn't happening. I was planning on moving back to Azerbaijan, where I grew up, and I didn't want to start anything.

The next day I received a bouquet of flowers with a note that said: "It's the possibility of a dream come true that makes life interesting." which is my favorite quote from the Alchemist by Paulo Coelho. There was no name on the note. I thought it was this other guy I went on a couple of dates with before, so I texted him to inquire if the flowers were from him. He texted back almost instantly saying: "No, the flowers are not from me. Sad face."

Only then I realized the flowers were from Alex and I felt so bad. I sent him a text immediately saying:"Sorry, I led you on. I don't think we're on the same page. I'm moving back to Azerbaijan. This is not happening." But he wouldn't give up! He sent me a text back saying, "No, let's just go out for a drink. We need to talk. I'm going to pick you up tonight after work."

Alex Was a Bingo

I was pleasantly surprised by Alex's reaction. I expected him to just give up. I was always drawn to Feminine Strength Males, but if I rejected them they'd almost instantly vanish. Deep down I wanted them to fight for me – to show their masculine energy. But they never did- until Alex. Alex was fighting. He knew what he wanted and he wasn't going to give up. He used his masculine energy to be a Bingo!

So he took me out again. We sat in a Bubble Tea shop and he kept talking to me about all the things he liked about me.

"Why are you trying so hard? Why? You know I'm moving away. There is no point to any of this," I said to him.

He looked me straight in the eyes and said, "Because I see it, Mimi. I see a vision of both of us. I see this working! ". He said it with so much love, sincerity and conviction that although I didn't admit it to him in that moment, I saw it too.

He made me fall in love with him. He conquered my heart with love and kindness—but he was proactive, not just wishing for it to happen.

I didn't say anything to him that evening, but I thought to myself, "Maybe he is right."

And so we started to go out, and it felt too good to be true. Most of us are conditioned to think that relationships need to be hard, and this one wasn't. It was so easy and fun to be with him that I would freak out once in a while and say, "No, this is too good to be true. It can't be real."

Whenever I ran away from him he came persistently and said, "What's going on? We had such a great time."

When he talked to me, he made me see our potential. He would state the obvious, and I would have nothing to say.

He was being the perfect Bingo: he was loving and kind (feminine) but determined and focused (masculine). He knew what he wanted and it was me. He wasn't aggressive or domineering—he was patient and strong. He was very certain.

Love is Feminine

For my part, I had to learn to bring out my feminine energy in a whole new way. Although I was already balanced in many ways. For example: I used my masculine energy to get a great job and was very successful financially, especially for my age. I also constantly exercised my feminine energy - I was very kind and caring to those around me. I always dressed up, mainly in pencil skirts and heels, hair and make up done. It all made me feel very good about myself. It made me feel whole and balanced.

But love required me to use my feminine energy in a way I had not done before. Truly loving somebody is all about using one's feminine energy. It requires you to let go of control and open up your heart. It's about relaxing, allowing and trusting.

It can be terrifying. I ran away from Alex three times before he calmed me down. Then, the more I opened up, the more I fell in love with him. There was nothing logical or rational about it, it was…well, magic.

Alex proposed when we were on a trip to Italy. We were in Positano, a beautiful village on the Amalfi coast. We were eating dinner outside. The stars were sparkling and the night was warm with a strong scent of orange trees. We decided to go for a walk on the beach. The full moon was shining bright, illuminating a beautiful reflection on the water and lighting the way for lovers.

He got down on one knee, and asked for me to be his partner for life. "The timing's not right," said my masculine energy. After all, we were both broke at the time and trying to figure out what we wanted to do with our lives. "Say 'Yes!' you love him and you will make things work," said my feminine energy. So I said *yes*. We got married exactly a year later.

Diving Into My Feminine Energy

As our relationship progressed I dived a bit too deep into feminine energy.

I started letting Alex take care of finances and make most of the decisions. For a short period of time, I lost myself completely. I was dwelling in a very emotional world. I stopped taking charge, of both myself and my life.

I became extremely miserable, unhappy, anxious and totally not in my element.

I realized that it wasn't making Alex happy either. Yes, he was stepping up and taking charge but he didn't want to be the boss all the time. He loved it when I was confident and in charge. For him, that was really sexy.

In trying to balance and be more feminine, I clearly went a bit too far. I completely disowned my strength—and that it not what The Bingo Theory is about. Yes, we must bring out our opposite energy. But we must always own our strengths. If we don't, it will rot inside of us.

Using Our Strengths

Eventually we both learned to use our strengths. I realized that Alex likes it when I use my masculine energy to make decisions and set plans. And I like it when he uses his feminine energy to bring the fun, love and spontaneity to our relationship.

It's even true in the little things, like decorating our house. Alex will do the research and say, "Should we get these plates or those plates or another plate?" He finds the options, and then I choose. He loves options. I love making decisions.

I wouldn't care enough to spend the hours looking for various options. I'd go to the first store, find something, get it, and forget about it. But at the same time I do enjoy being surrounded by beautiful things, that were well thought of and put together. I would hardly ever sit down and light candles and put on music and create an atmosphere. Sometimes, when I'm alone I eat in the kitchen standing up. But Alex makes everything special. For him, that comes naturally. And the best part is that he brings that out of me too.

Learn From Each Other

We're always learning how to find greater balance within ourselves from each other.

When Alex and I have arguments, he is very expressive. He openly shares his feelings and emotions with me. Once he is done talking, he usually looks at me and says: " What are you thinking about?"

For him, it's easy to express himself. He processes his emotions very fast. For me on the other hand, it's much harder. I don't always know how to communicate what's going on internally. Heck, half of the time I don't even know what's going on internally. It takes time for me to absorb information and be able to express my internal reaction to a given situation. I usually respond by saying, "Umm… I have nothing to say" or "I need some time to absorb what I have just heard".

I've had to learn to express myself better, and Alex has had to learn to give me time to respond. Sometimes it only takes a few minutes and sometimes it can take up to half an hour or longer. With his help I've learned to use my feminine energy more. I've become more expressive, more loving and more compassionate towards myself and others.

As for Alex, he's able to step into his masculine energy when he needs to. He stands up to me when I get bossy and will take a tough line when I need him to. After we got married and I was going too far into my feminine energy he was the one who was adamant that I find a way to help myself. "You have to do something about this. Only you have the power to get yourself out of this black hole." Eventually I ended up going to a silent meditation retreat and Alex was a huge part in supporting and encouraging me to do it. He wasn't going to allow me to stay down.

We're continually helping each other to become more balanced. We're evolving as humans.

Sexual Attraction

Some people worry that if both people in the relationship embrace both their masculine and feminine energies, then the men and women will become the same. The sexual spark will go away because there is no polarity. That's not true.

Our strength energies are different, so we will always have the attraction of opposites. What's more, when you accept and embrace both the masculine and feminine sides of yourself, you can explore and share both of these sides of yourself.

There are times when I take on the masculine role and initiate sex and then there are times when Alex does. There are times when he is the strong dominant force and times when I am. We swap. We play. Our relationship is all encompassing. There is passion and tenderness. Excitement and peace. Closeness and freedom.

Our relationship is about more than adhering to certain roles, it is bigger than that. It's about learning about ourselves and sharing that learning with each other. It is about being happy and connected—not just for our sake, but for the sake of everyone around us.

Once you are a fulfilled in yourself and within your partnership—*truly* fulfilled—then you can stop looking inwards.

Then you're not just thinking of yourself or your relationships; you can start to think about the world around you. What can you do to help others? How can you share your love with the world? This is where the journey really begins.

TIPS FOR A BINGO RELATIONSHIP
How do you find a Bingo relationship? How do you find

a Bingo partner if you are single? Or how do you make an existing relationship into a Bingo relationship? Well, it all starts with you. *It always starts with you.*

Once you start to balance your own masculine and feminine energies you will attract someone who is equally balanced. Like attracts like.

If you're in a relationship and you've been balancing your energies and working on yourself, what does that mean for your partner? Is she also changing? Does he resent the changes you've made? Is she becoming more balanced herself?

We mimic what we see. If you're working on yourself, it could be that your partner is consciously—or unconsciously— changing too.

You can't change your partner; you can only change yourself. Then you can lead by example. When you get more balanced, they may get inspired to be balance as well.

If your partner doesn't balance, it's up to you to choose whether to accept it or not. Does this relationship still work for you? Are you helping each other grow?

Although you cannot change someone else, you can respectfully tell them how you feel. For example, if your Masculine Strength partner isn't talking to you about how he or she feels then gently and kindly challenge them to share with you. Encourage them to open up, ask more questions. Explain how much you love it when they tell you about their day. If they are being aggressive, then explain that they can get so much further with you when they are patient and understanding. Likewise, if your Feminine Strength Partner is getting needy and emotional, remind them that they are strong, that they are not victims, they can do anything. Help them to be more decisive and to take charge. Encourage them.

You can't force someone to change but you can help you partner grow—if they're open to that. That's what relationships are for. And if one partner doesn't want to grow, then you have to question whether it is still a relationship that works for you.

Having a Bingo relationship is something we are always working at; it's a constant journey, not an end-destination.

CHAPTER XXI

CONCLUSION:
THE BIGGER BINGO

ON A DECEMBER morning in 1996, a Harvard trained brain-scientist woke up with a pounding pain behind her left eye. It was the kind of headache you get after eating too much ice cream. Not sure what was going on, Jill Bolte Taylor tried to go about her day as she normally would. She stepped on to her exercise machine and started to work out but the headache was getting worse. She looked down at her hands on the bars and they looked liked "claws". She felt odd.

She got off the machine and started to walk across her living room floor when she realized that everything was slowing down. She could almost hear her mind telling her muscles to contract and relax, but they were not obeying instructions.

She lost her balance and leaned against the wall. As she did that, she had the strange sensation that she could not define where she ended and where the wall began. "The atoms and the molecules of my arm blended with the atoms and molecules of the wall," she later said. "All I could detect was this energy... energy."

Her mind was desperately trying to make sense of what was happening – but then it stopped completely. There was silence. Suddenly she felt "enormous and expansive... at one with all the energy that was, and it was beautiful there."

She felt a state of euphoria.

At that moment her right arm became totally paralyzed, and her brain chatter started again – it told her "I am having a stroke!"

Some of you may have seen Dr Bolte Taylor's fascinating TED talk, in which she describes with amazing detail what it felt like as the left side of her brain slowly closed down, leaving her reliant on just the right side of her brain.

As I explained in the opening chapter, it's believed that the left side of our brain specializes in logic, rationality, language, rules and strategy. The right side of our brain is where we get our creativity, imagination, curiosity and intuition.

Of course, nothing is as simple and clean-cut as that. There is always a complex interaction between the two sides of the brain—which is why the idea that you are either "left brained" or "right brained" has been disputed. However, the basic principle that each hemisphere assimilates the world in a different way holds true.

Eastern philosophies have always argued that our left brain is our masculine energy, and the right is our feminine.

Quite suddenly, Dr Bolte Taylor was living almost entirely in her feminine energy. She says it was Nirvana.

"When we see life through the right hemisphere," Dr Bolte Taylor continued saying, "we see that we are energy beings connected to one another...We are brothers and sisters on this planet, here to make the world a better place. And in this moment we are perfect, we are whole and we are beautiful."

This feeling of connectedness and of beauty was so heavenly that she found it hard to leave it. But she knew that if she wanted to survive, she needed to get help— and for that, she would need her left hemisphere, her masculine side. She needed to use what was left of her linear, logical numerical thinking in order to pick up the phone and get help. And fortunately she managed to make that call and help arrived before the clot in her brain totally stopped the left hemisphere from functioning.

I cannot think of a stronger story to demonstrate the importance of having both the masculine intellect and the feminine intuition. Without the masculine energy to pick up that phone, Dr. Bolte Taylor would have died, and yet, by getting in touch with her pure feminine energy, she experienced the "life-force power of the universe."

In this book we've seen how important it is to balance our masculine and feminine energies for the sake of our own fulfillment and contentment. We've seen how, once you start to achieve that balance, you can have beautiful relationships with others. Relationships in which you share your love without always wanting something in return. Relationships that help you grow and evolve as a human being.

"The repression of the feminine has led to a planet on the edge of collapse. The re-emergence is going to be a dance to behold"

— CLARE DAKIN

Beyond You

Now I want to share the bigger picture with you. Yes, The Bingo Theory will bring you more happiness and love, but it can also change the world. Does that sound over the top? It's not.

I believe that everything that's wrong with the world—everything that's imbalanced and every conflict—comes from an inability to balance our masculine and feminine energies.

Balancing our energy is therefore not just a personal matter. It's vital for the survival of our species and the survival of our planet. Not just you, not just me, but collectively we need to balance our masculine and feminine energies.

Why? Well, look at what is happening in the world at the moment.

We live in a world that's run by the masculine energy.

Status, competition, money, ambition, capitalism and power are the masculine values in the world today. We are told that growth matters above all else. We go to war, we invade, we expand, we dominate.

But at what cost?

We're disconnected from nature. We are running out of space. We are running out of trees. The number of endangered species is through the roof. We are disconnected not just from the land we live on but from other people. Man is killing fellow man.

We're told that the masculine ideal of financial success will make us happy, but what is success? Being successful is about being fulfilled in yourself and in your relationships with your loved ones— as well as being accomplished in your business or career.

From day to day, does all of our economic growth bring us happiness or health? And if it doesn't, then what's the point? It's great to have a business - I have several myself - but you have to keep asking yourself the bigger questions: Am I happy? Am I connected? Am I loving?

We can't blame just the masculine energy, though. We also see extremes of the feminine energy which can be superficial and irresponsible. It is our extreme feminine energy that is irresponsible enough to keep consuming. We want more, more, more with no thought to where it's coming from or who has been hurt to provide it. We think that happiness lies in the next shopping trip, but it doesn't. You only need to looks at rates of depression in the United States to see that.

The reality is that you have to decide for yourself what makes you happy. At the end of the day, true happiness comes first from having a good relationship with yourself, a better relationship with other people, and then an even better relationship with the world.

I believe that any human being can be balanced, it's in our nature. It's actually our conditioning that makes us unbalanced.

Right now we need more feminine energy in the world. We need more love, connection, and empathy. We need to love ourselves, love our fellow man and love this beautiful planet we live on and all of its inhabitants, whose survival depends on us.

But we can't lose the masculine energy. The masculine is needed to get things done. The feminine energy cries for what's happening to the planet but does nothing about it. We need the masculine energy to take action and make change.

When we combine the feminine heart with masculine action, we can change the world. I not only believe that. I *know* that. We can live in peaceful co-existence, man, woman and nature. We can live in a way that is sustainable yet progressive.

And we already have that within us. We have both the masculine and the feminine. The left brain and the right brain. We have the power to choose which energy to use and when to use it. From moment to moment we choose.

Now is the time to do this. You're ready. We need this balance in order to survive.

BONUS SECTION

The Bingo Career

.....

BONUS SECTION:
THE BINGO CAREER

ONE OF THE MOST powerful ways you can balance yourself is to have a career that allows you to develop your less
dominant energy. After all, most of us spend the majority
of our day working. If you have a very strong masculine
energy, it will help you to work in a profession that brings
out your feminine energy. And if you have a very strong
feminine energy, it will help you if you take a role that
encourages you to bring out your masculine energy.

Think about what energy you use more every day. Does
it make you more balanced or less balanced? Are you giv-
en the opportunity to use your less dominant energy?

If you're only relying on your strength energy you
might be unhappy. For example, I used to work in a
bank. It was a very logical, masculine environment.
Staying at the bank I would only develop more of my
masculine energy.

Now that Alex and I have our own businesses, my favorite part involves creating content such as videos and

photos. This helps me to be creative and to express myself. It also helps me connect to others. It brings out my feminine energy.

You don't necessarily have to quit your job, however. You can probably find ways to use different energies within your existing role. For example, if you're a Masculine Strength Person who works in a bank then see if you can get involved with training new staff or being a mentor. This will bring out your caring, connected feminine energy.

If you are a Feminine Strength Person working in a creative, feminine field, see if there is anything you can do to use your masculine energy. Can you take responsibility for some of the finances? Can you start a new project that gives you the opportunity to show leadership and take on responsibilities?

In this bonus section, you'll find some career ideas for both the Masculine and Feminine Strength Person.

CHAPTER XXII

THE BINGO CAREER FOR FEMININE STRENGTH PEOPLE

IF YOU'RE a Feminine Strength Male or Female it will help you to work in a profession that calls on you to use your masculine energy. This could be anything to do with science, systems, numbers, finance, business, or construction.

While these might not seem like a natural fit, they will help you to stretch yourself and develop your weaker energy. For example, I have a good friend who is a Feminine Strength Female who writes for a business website. This job allows her to use her natural feminine energy to express and communicate, but the subject matter she deals with is very logical, clear and masculine in its energy. That job is a Bingo.

It might surprise you but Feminine Strength People are great law enforcers. This is because they have natural empathy and compassion, that can help diffuse difficult situations. They won't stray into aggression but they do have to step into their power.

For the feminine energy, it's good to work for yourself.

This experience teaches them how to be independent and run their own show. They can feel strong and in control. However, the problem the feminine energy usually faces is in monetizing their talent. They usually charge too little—the feminine energy does not tend to value itself highly and this often results in a constant struggle to make ends meet. The term "starving artist" often describes a very talented Feminine Strength Person who is incapable of making an income from their genius. It's often a good idea for these people to have a Masculine Strength business partner or manager.

Another challenge for Feminine Strength People is acting on all the great ideas they have. They are constantly torn in many directions because they usually possess talents in many fields. This makes it harder for them to decide which steps to take. Again, a masculine energy business partner will help you do that too.

- **SCIENCE**—You might have assumed that scientists are all Masculine Strength People. But the great ones start out from love of nature, fascination with the world, and curiosity about how things work. These are qualities of the feminine energy. However, to get ahead in the field, you need to be doggedly persistent, logical, objective, rational, self-motivated and organized—in other words, you need to use your masculine energy. This makes science a great Bingo career.

- **FINANCE** – To succeed in the financial field you need to engage in logical and analytical thinking, be good at problem-solving, have strong numerical skills, and be able to manage your time and lead others, all of which use your masculine energy. However, your natural feminine strengths of communication, teamwork and humility will be vital too. The financial world today is the product of too much masculine energy and this has resulted in risk taking, macho competition and reckless decisions. Now more than ever the financial industry needs the feminine energy.

- **SELF-EMPLOYED**—Being self-employed forces you to sell yourself, to be confident in your abilities, to organize your time, and place a value on your work. This can be a challenge for Feminine Strength People but it will also be hugely rewarding and a great way to become balanced.

- **LAW ENFORCEMENT** – Working with the law will bring out feelings of strength, certainty and power— all masculine energy. But your natural strengths of empathy and communication will be invaluable too.

- **FILM MAKER**—creating a piece of art on film is a very feminine energy. But the decision making process of editing it, shaping it, and finishing it is a very masculine energy.

CHAPTER XXIII

THE BINGO CAREER FOR MASCULINE STRENGTH PEOPLE

IF YOU HAVE a strong masculine energy, it will be great for you to find work that helps you develop your feminine, caring, creative energy.

I have a Masculine Strength Friend - Paula, who used to work as an investment banker. In her late 20s, she was on her way to being made the youngest partner in her bank. She was phenomenally successful. Then she had a car crash, which made her re-evaluate her whole life. Paula quit her job and went travelling. She decided to become a nutritionist. She was the top of her game in a male-dominant environment, but she left it all behind.

Now Paula presents cooking shows. She's taken her drive and ambition and applied it in a completely different area. She loves what she does and feels a lot happier; she has a sense of purpose. Paula was great at what she did before. She was very successful in a highly competitive industry, but it didn't bring her joy. She did it because it came effortlessly to her. Now she's using her natural business skills, but in a new way. She's also constantly challenging herself to learn and grow. She uses her creativity to create recipes that she shares in here cooking show, as well as her blog, she educates people about proper nutrition which helps them live healthier lifestyles, and since she is in the public eye, she is constantly challenged to express herself and become a better communicator. Practicing this daily, as this is her job, helps her keep a healthy balance between her masculine and feminine energy.

I have another friend who's a very logical guy and he's become a great teacher. It works for him because it brings out his caring, empathetic side. Being a Masculine Strength Male helps him tremendously in his role, as his is not overly emotional so he doesn't get too upset or manipulated by the kids. He's strong and dominant, which makes him a great teacher. He has their attention and he uses compassion and leadership.

Nursing and medicine are great career choices for Masculine Strength People. It allows them to express their caring side; however, their masculine logic and detachment mean that they are always calm enough to do their job well.

Believe it or not a lot of fashion designers are Masculine Strength People. They go into the creative field because it makes them feel more balanced. They might not have consciously chosen it for this reason— they may just know that it makes them feel good. In fact, the question to always ask about any job (and anything else for that matter) is: "Does this make me feel good?". If it doesn't, it might be time to change things up.

Jobs that will bring out your feminine energy:

- **CREATIVE WORK** —Work in art, design and fashion will help you get in touch with your creative, imaginative, aesthetic feminine energy. The feminine energy lives for beauty and sees it everywhere; having a creative job will help you to see this beauty. Your natural strengths will allow you to make it financially successful. Feminine Strength People might have fantastic creative talents but they struggle to monetize their talent.

- **TEACHING** – This work will bring out your caring, nurturing, patient feminine energy. It will also allow you to draw on your natural strengths—being strong, confident, disciplined, authoritative and structured in the classroom.

- **HEALTHCARE JOBS** —Nursing and medicine will allow you to work on your empathetic, caring side. In these jobs your natural masculine strength will allow you to stay detached enough to do the job well. If you get too emotionally involved with all your patients, you will burn out.

- **SOCIAL WORK**—Counseling is a human profession that relies on the feminine energy of connectedness, communication, empathy and caring. At the same time, your masculine strength will help you to stay strong and focused enough to deal with the practicalities.

- **WORKING WITH ANIMALS OR CHILDREN**—The masculine energy is well suited to being a vet or a pediatrician. Working with animals and children will help you connect to your loving, caring and playful side. Your natural masculine detachment and logic will mean you don't become overly emotional with your work.

REFERENCES

.....

CHAPTER 1
Yin and Yang story
Bierlein, J.F, *Parallel Myths*, Random House Publishing Group, 16 Jun 2010

Simon Baron Cohen, Empathizing and Systemizing Brain
Macrae, Fiona - Do you have a male or female brain? How women could earn more by thinking like men, *Daily Mail*, 30 October 2015
Mosley, Michael, Do you have a male or female brain? The simple test that investigates your 'gender personality'... and the answer will surprise you, *Daily Mail*, 26 April 2015,
BBC One, Horizon asked Professor Alice Roberts
BBC.com, Sex ID, Brain Sex, Science: Human Mind and Body
Stains, Laurence Roy, Why Men Need to Show Emotion, Men's Health, September 13, 2006

A Unique Mosaic
Rumbelow, Helen, Why there is no such thing as a Female brain, *The Times*, December 2 2015
Hamzelou, Jessica, Brains are not male or female, *New Scientist*, December 5 2015

Societal pressures
Holloway, Kali, Masculinity Is Killing Men: The Roots
of Men and Trauma. AlterNet.com
June 6, 2015

CHAPTER 2
The Finger Test
Manning, John, Digit Ratio, Faber and Faber 2009
Mosley Michael, The tests that show if you've got a male
or female brain: The answer may surprise you - and
explain your personality, *Daily Mail*, 30 September 2014
Hanlon, Michael, What the length of your index finger
says about you, *Daily Mai*l, 3 December 2010

CHAPTERS 4-7
The physical characteristics of the 4 types as shaped by
testosterone and estrogen
Angier, Natalie, Male Hormone Molds Women, Too, In
Mind and Body, New York Times, May 3, 1994
Burne, Jerome, What a man can't resist: the perfect
waist-hip ratio, *Independent*, 3 October 1994
Highfield, Roger, Attractive women are more than just
a pretty face, *Telegraph*, 02 Nov 2005
Pincott, Jena, Sex, science and the art of seduction:
What really makes us attractive to the opposite sex,
Daily Mail, 8 October 2008
Why the 'Perfect' Body isn't always perfect: How Hor-
mones interact with Waist-to-hip ratios in Women,
University of Chicago Press Journals, December 5, 2008

CHAPTER 8
Cinderella
Cinderella, Kenneth Branagh and Chris Weitz, Walt
Disney, 2015

Leonardo Da Vinci was a Bingo
Papova, Maria, Leonardo's Brain: What a Posthumous
Brain Scan Six Centuries Later Reveals about the
Source of Da Vinci's Creativity, Brainpickings.com, ref-
erencing Leonardo's Brain: Understanding Da Vinci's
Creative Genius, by Leonard Shlain
Papova, Maria, Why 'Psychological Androgyny' is
Essential for Creativity, Brainpickings.com referencing
Creativity, The Psychology of Discovery and Invention,
Mihaly Csikszentmihalyi
Bergland, Christopher, Einstein's Genius Linked to
Well-Connected Brain Hemispheres, psychologytoday.
com, October 05, 2013.

CHAPTER 9: How to become a Bingo for Feminine
Strength Female or Male
Vigorous Exercise
Mercola, Joseph, 9 Body Hacks to Naturally Increase
Testosterone, mercola.com, July 27 2012.

Power Pose
Cuddy, Amy, Your Body Language Shapes you are Are,
Ted.com, June 2012

Power Dress
Bridge, Sarah, why simply putting on exercise gear will make you WANT to work out - and means you will get better results too, Mail on Sunday, 16 December 2013
Get Your Hands Dirty
Davidson, Jacob, Chopping Wood: a Manlier feel than Sports, TIME, August 26th 2013

CHAPTER 10: How to become a Bingo for Feminine Strength Female or Male

Express
Hagan, Pat, Don't bottle up your emotions – it'll knock years off your life and raise cancer risk by 70 percent, Daily Mail, September 7 2013

Spend time alone
Bourg Carter, Sherrie, Reasons You Should Spend More Time Alone: The Healthy Aspects of Solitude, psychologytoday.com Jan 31, 2012

Get a massage
Rabin, Roni Caryn, Regimens: Massage Benefits Are More Than Skin Deep, New York Times, September 20, 2010, Macrae, Fiona, Cuddle hormone holds the secret to looking beautiful: Whiff of oxytocin makes men find their partners more attractive, 26 November 2013

Take a Nap
Barker, Eric, Why you should really take a nap this afternoon, according to science, The Week, July 25, 2014

Get a pet

Sample, Ian, Dogs are man's best friend thanks to bonding hormone, research shows, The Guardian, April 16, 2015

Skerrett, Patrick J, Pets can help their humans create friendships, find social support, Harvard Health, October 29 2015

Scott, Sophie, 10 things you may not know about laughter, bbc.com, 26 October 2016

Dress Up

Bridge, Sarah, Why simply putting on exercise gear will make you WANT to work out - and means you will get better results too, Mail on Sunday, 16 December 2013

Be in Nature

Reynolds, Gretchen, How Walking in Nature Changes the Brain New York Times, July 22, 2015

Acupuncture

Christian, Nordqvist, How does acupuncture work? Medicalnewstoday.com 21 December 2015

Read fiction

Bury, Liz Reading literary fiction improves empathy, study finds, guardian.com, 8 October 2013

Listen to music

Griffiths, Sarah, Feeling down? Then listen to SAD music: Melancholy tunes lift our moods, Daily Mail, November 4 2014

CHAPTER 11: Bingo Relationships
The Magical Kitchen
Ruiz, Don Miguel, *The Mastery of Love*, Amber-Allen
Publishing, Inc, 1999

PART VII: The Bigger Bingo
Bolte-Taylor, Jill, My stroke of insight, ted.com, March
2008

BIBLIOGRAPHY

.....

Allen, Patricia, *Getting to 'I do': The Secret to Doing Relationships Right!* Harper Collins, New York, 1994

Deida, David *The Way of the Superior Man: A Spiritual Guide to Mastering the Challenges of Women, Work and Sexual desire*, Sounds True, Boulder, Colorado, 1997, 2004

Gawain, Shakti, *The Shakti Gawain Essentials: 3 Books in 1: Creative Visualization, Living in the Light and Developing Intuition*, Kindle Edition

Gray, John, *Men Are from Mars, Women Are from Venus: A Practical Guide for Improving Communication and Getting What You Want in Your Relationships: How to Get What You Want in Your Relationships*, HarperCollins, New York 1992

Moir, Anne & David Jessel *Brain Sex: The Real Difference between Men and Women*, Michael Joseph, London, 1989

Pease, Allan & Barbara, *Why Men Don't Listen and Women Can't Read Map*, Orion, London, 1999

Rhodes, Sonya & Shneider, Susan, *The Alpha Woman Meets Her Match: How today's strong women can find love and happiness without settling*, HarperCollins, New York 2014

Ruiz, Don Miguel, *The Mastery of Love*, Amber-Allen Publishing, Inc, 1999